$3.50

Modern Viking

The Story of Abraham Vereide, Pioneer in Christian Leadership

by Norman Grubb

᠁thor of *The Liberating Secret, The Law of Faith, Touching the Invisible,* etc.

This is the fascinating story of the Inter-᠁tional Christian Leadership Movement ᠁d its founder, Dr. Abraham Vereide. ᠁C. L. is known around the world es-᠁cially for its sponsorship of the annual ᠁esidential Breakfasts in Washington, ᠁C., and this book contains many inter-᠁ting sidelights on these famous events ᠁d personalities.

᠁Political leaders in Washington are ᠁arm in their praise of Dr. Vereide and ᠁s work:

᠁Senator Alexander Wiley says of Dr. ᠁ereide, "He has brought to countless ᠁mbers of men an awakening to the ᠁iritual verities, and his influence, as ᠁own in a number of places, has made ᠁r cleaner politics and better living."

᠁Congressman Charles E. Bennett says, ᠁braham Vereide originally envisioned ᠁is Group—the House Breakfast Group ᠁hich meets every Thursday morning for ᠁ayer, discussion and Christian fellow-᠁ip — the most significant thing I know ᠁ Capitol Hill. I consider him to be one ᠁ America's greatest citizen-leaders and ᠁e of our Master's greatest tools for ᠁od."

᠁"Reading the life story of Abraham ᠁ereide is like boarding a fast-moving ᠁ain," writes the reviewer in *Faith at ᠁ork* magazine, "for here is a man who ᠁s been hurtling through life since child-᠁od and now, in his mid-seventies, is ᠁ll going strong. Though Vereide is Nor-᠁egian by birth, it is difficult to think of ᠁m except as the American pioneer, and ᠁e various stages and episodes in his ᠁e epitomize the best of the forces that ᠁aped this nation.

(continued from front flap)

"The story of the development of International Christian Leadership is only slightly less interesting than the story of Vereide himself. And the names that dot the pages!—presidents of the United States, kings and queens, French diplomats, members of Parliament, African and Indian leaders, millionaires, governors, and great Christians of all kinds: Graham, Sunday, Peter Marshall, Schweitzer, Shoemaker, Peale. No less interesting are the anonymous men and women whose stories gleam thorugh the swift-paced narrative: the mining camp rowdies, alcoholics, taxi-drivers, churchmen. All in all, this volume is a significant achievement."

Modern
Viking

MODERN
VIKING

The Story of Abraham Vereide,
Pioneer in Christian Leadership

by
NORMAN GRUBB

ZONDERVAN PUBLISHING HOUSE
GRAND RAPIDS   MICHIGAN

21297

FOREWORD

Senator Frank Carlson
Senator Alexander Wiley
Judge Boyd Leedom
Congressman Charles E. Bennett

U. S. Senate
Washington, D. C.
September 26, 1960

Abraham Vereide is one of the choice souls who has dedicated and devoted his life to the cause of the Master. His background, his character, and his personality have made him a recognized Christian leader among all faiths. His life has been an inspiration to me.

The I.C.L. and many other fine programs he has sponsored and worked on will remain as a monument to him. His life's work has been a blessing to all.

FRANK CARLSON

U. S. Senate
Committee on Foreign Relations
September 13, 1960

I am very happy to say a few words about Abraham Vereide. I remember some fifteen years ago or so when he came to town. He came up to see me and he suggested then the "breakfast meetings." He spoke of his success in the West, and, of course, he has been going strong ever since.

I think he is one of the finest Christian gentlemen I have ever met and he is dedicated to his job. He has brought to countless numbers of men an awakening to the spiritual verities, and his influence, as shown in a number of places, has made for cleaner politics and better living.

ALEXANDER WILEY

National Labor Relations Board
Washington, D. C.
September 16, 1960
As Christ became more significant in my life, I developed a desire, almost subconsciously, to seek out men who best personified Christ as I understood Him. Abraham Vereide is such a man. I presume the fine qualities I observe in him, day in and day out, both in times of thrilling success and in discouraging difficulties, emanate from his love for God and his brothers. Kindly, tolerant, and understanding in all situations, he seems never to be separated far from the source he recognizes as his strength, the Spirit of Christ. At times when I have really needed it, I have never failed to get help from Christ through Abram.

BOYD LEEDOM

Congress of the United States
House of Representatives
Washington, D. C.
March 21, 1961
The House Breakfast Group, meeting every Thursday morning for prayer, religious discussion, and Christian fellowship, is the most significant thing I know of on Capital Hill.
It has brought a richer understanding of important Scriptures. It has tested our individual actions by sharpening our consciences. It has approached great individual and national crises with prayers of soul searching, dedication, and commitment. It has helped us to grow in spirit by giving testimony of individual problems met and partly or wholly surmounted. Greatly treasured by most of us is the warm friendship which has developed among us at these meetings.
Worthy of much praise is Abraham Vereide, who originally envisioned this group and who has been a constant, effective, and friendly support to it. I consider him to be one of America's greatest citizen leaders and one of our Master's greatest tools for good.

CHARLES E. BENNETT, M.C.

PREFACE

I have been honored by the invitation to write this life of Abraham Vereide. It has been no duty task, but very much a labor of love, because fifteen years of ever closer association with him have continually deepened my love and respect for him. I am paying no idle compliment when I say that association with him and his co-workers in International Christian Leadership is something I have greatly prized and by which I have greatly benefited.

The preparation of his life has been an eye-opener to me. I knew him as a man with a great love for God and his fellow-men, and a man of far-reaching vision; but I by no means realized the depth and fullness of the currents of inner devotion and ceaseless dedication to his great commission as a servant of and witness to Jesus Christ which flowed in him.

Though given the name of Abraham Vereide, he has usually been called Abram, and I use this shortened form throughout the book; I also occasionally call him, as some do, by his initials, A.V. International Christian Leadership is likewise known and commonly called by its initials I.C.L.

I believe in letting a man tell his own story as far as possible, so I have not been reticent in the use of quotations, especially in the account of his early life, which he had written himself. I came upon the treasure trove of the book, at least as far as knowing the real heart-beat of A.V., when his wife was persuaded to loan me some two hundred of his letters to her while he was in the process of launching International Christian Leadership in Washington, and both were feeling the heat of the battle. I could not get him very interested in the preparation of the book at first, and I don't blame him. It was a matter of catching a shy fish; but when I read him extracts of those letters during three quiet days I had with him, then he seemed

7

to wake up and warm up to the possibilities of this book for glorifying his Saviour, not himself, and he gave me many useful anecdotes as we went over the manuscript together.

Others have helped much. Mrs. Aymar Johnson, who has been with Mr. and Mrs. Vereide from the early days of I.C.L., spent days with her co-worker, Miss Ann Gill, going through masses of papers and letters, and has followed along with me all the way. Mr. Vereide's daughter, Alicia Abrahamsen, who is heart and soul in the work with him, gave me much also, with her steady backing and often apt and balancing comments. Wallace Haines of the I.C.L. in Europe has given me much too, and others, all of whom I could not mention.

In the preparation of the book, a friend in Toronto, Miss Rebecca Fleming, kindly lent me an apartment in her home where I could be completely quiet, and where I was looked after by her assistant, Miss Anne Lyons. One of my co-workers, Mr. Cliff Bartlett, gave me two weeks of voluntary help with the typing, for which I was very grateful.

I am thankful to Senator Frank Carlson and Senator Alexander Wiley of the United States Senate, the Hon. Charles E. Bennett of the House of Representatives, and Judge Boyd Leedom, Chairman of the Labor Relations Board, for their words of introduction.

I am sure that I shall echo Abraham Vereide's own hope when I say that the aim of this book is to point beyond a man or movement to Him who alone is "the Way, the Truth and the Life" for the world.

NORMAN GRUBB

CONTENTS

LIST OF ILLUSTRATIONS

Modern
Viking

PROLOGUE

President Eisenhower walked through a crowded breakfast room in the Ballroom of the Mayflower Hotel in Washington. The date was February, 1960. The guests, numbering about 900, were standing. They included many of the nation's leaders: secretaries of state, senators and congressmen, chiefs of staff, judges of the Supreme Court and foreign ambassadors of various nations.

Following him out of the room was a broad-shouldered, upright, white-haired man, with ruddy countenance, striking features, and blue eyes, who himself might have been one of the senators or ambassadors. As the President said goodbye to this man at the hotel entrance, he remarked that this was the best breakfast that they had yet had. Overstaying his time by twenty minutes, although he was due at a Security Council meeting, the President had been listening to various speakers— a newspaper owner from Los Angeles, a Metropolitan Opera singer, a British member of Parliament, a senator, and a congressman, telling that distinguished audience in simple language of the change in their lives and the effect in their homes and in their business and political activities, since they made a personal commitment of themselves to Jesus Christ.

1 | THE YOUNG VIKING

Back on the rugged mountain slopes of Norway years before, a little fellow of eight was taking the cattle to pasture one June morning. He was the same one who now accompanied the President and who was responsible for this unusual breakfast.

The young lad had recently lost his mother, and an indescribable loneliness possessed him; for no one but she had understood and loved and helped him with his Viking nature, which had so often brought him into "fights and fury."

"I had closed the gate behind me," he told in after years, "when this hunger for Mother and for release from the tempest that raged within, and for deliverance from guilt and passion, took hold of me. I hurried into the thicket of elder trees near the brook in a secluded spot, where I threw myself on the ground to cry my heart out and pray. I had a hunch that God was yonder, but I knew so little about Him, or what He had accomplished on our behalf by sending His Son into the world to give His life a ransom for us; but I did know that I was a naughty boy and that I wanted to be good. As I prayed, I had a vivid consciousness of a Divine Presence and into my mind flashed a statement that I later discovered was from Isaiah 43:1: 'Fear not, for I have redeemed thee and called thee by name, thou art mine.'

"I accepted that, not knowing what it meant but that God had undertaken for me, and I yielded Him my all, so far as I knew. With it came a sense of release, of peace and joy. I rose to my feet, and as I looked around, everything seemed to be so beautiful, the moss, the grass, the trees, the leaves, the sky above me, everything had taken on a different hue. An ugly old man, who had been terribly mean to us boys, came to mind, but even he appeared different and I felt that I loved him and forgave him; in fact, that I could love everybody. A verse came to my

13

12-35-10 Gloppen. Vereide.

The village of Vereide, Norway. His home is the house in the center of the picture.

mind and I began to sing, 'O think what a wonder, I am God's own son.'

"I rushed home to tell others about it. Father was sitting in a rocking chair, reading a paper. I rushed toward him and said, 'Dad, I believe I am a Christian.' At that time he didn't know what a Christian experience meant, so he didn't pay any attention to me. I climbed up on his knees and brushed the paper aside, took hold of his side whiskers (he was smooth-shaven on lips and chin), and looked into those clear blue-grey eyes under those heavy eyebrows and that stern, yet kind face, and I shook his head and said, 'It's real, Dad, it's real!' 'That's good, my boy,' said he, and set me gently off his knees, to go on reading his paper.

"That did not satisfy. I must tell others who would understand and who would respond, so I found my playmates. There were Rasmus, Knut, Soren, Olaf, Mons, Per, Lars. They had to hear the story. I reminded them that they, too, had stolen those apples; they, too, had rolled the rocks down the steep hill against the cottage of the poor man below; they, too, had told stories; they, too, needed to be forgiven and to pray. I thought they had to come the same way as I did, and insisted that they lie down on the ground and pray. Some responded and some laughed, but three of the boys were in earnest and found that God condescends to meet us where we are and makes Himself known to us according to our capacity."

This young lad's home was in one of the world's beauty spots, up a charming inlet of the Nordfjord, on Norway's west coast between Bergen and Trondheim. The Gloppenfjord inlet is an eight mile long beauty spot presenting a never-to-be-forgotten picture of scenic grandeur, snow-covered peaks, deep valleys, lakes and rivers, summer pastures for thriving cattle, forest-covered mountain slopes, a long stretch of choice farms with their white farmhouses and red barns, where every home has a tall flagpole with the red, white, and blue of the Norwegian flag waving on it, and the well-kept highway running along the bay on either side.

At the end of the fjord lies the picturesque village of Sandane. Halfway up, the steamer from Bergen or Moldoy makes a stop. The place is called Vereide. A village store with a well-ordered supply of merchandise, a telephone exchange, a bakery, a small industry, a post office, and a white stone church surrounded by a cemetery greets our gaze as we approach the dock. Historically, the name of the place goes back to 963 A.D.

In that church the lad had been christened and confirmed in the Lutheran faith, following the tradition of his forebears who for generations back were buried in the graveyard outside.

The church was the meeting place for people from far and wide. Even trade and bartering were carried on there. On a beautiful Sunday morning it was a colorful scene, with boats of every description coming from various directions, and people afoot and in carriage or buggy, all streaming towards the house of God to worship, to pray, and to unite in the singing of the hymns that have brought comfort and inspiration to young and old.

"A short distance up the hill, we came to the level fields, gardens, stately birch, oak, maple, and horse chestnut trees, and to the impressive white Vereide *prestegaard*, the clergyman's residence. Nearby was a humbler house, with thatched roof, surrounded by an inviting garden. This peaceful spot was my birthplace and my home for eighteen years," writes Abram Vereide of his early years.

"Father had been one of three, and later the only supervisor and operator, of this vast state-owned property. He and his godly wife were happily surrounded by four splendid daughters, but they had prayed and longed for a son. On a bright October morning, the seventh, of 1886, the news was announced that Anders and Helene had a son. Mother said that he was dedicated to God before he was born."

When he was christened, the best people in the community were chosen for godfathers and godmothers and, according to custom, he was to be named after his grandfathers on both sides—Anders Elias. When the venerable clergyman came to the part of the ritual where he asked what the baby should be called, he was dissatisfied with the name and protested. He left the baptismal font and the small group gathered about it and walked down the crowded church to locate the father, to seek his consent to the name of Abraham. Returning to the elevated font of the church for the continuance of the sacred rite, he announced in a resounding voice, "Abraham, I baptize

16

thee in the name of the Father, the Son, and the Holy Spirit."
So the boy was called Abraham Vereide.

The last he remembered of his mother was when she had him
kneel at her bedside while she put her hands on him in prayer.
Her prayer was that God would deliver him from his uncon-
trollable temper and make him a real Christian. The answer
was given that June morning, and through the Scripture which
came to the young lad's mind, he joined that great host of those
who have been "begotten again of the lively Word."

In an unusual way his experience of his encounter with God
and his assurance of Christ as his personal Saviour seemed to
meet the need of young and old in that country community. It
was like a spark in a pile of firewood. Perhaps it was with them
as with many sincere churchgoers—a faith in a God of history
rather than a contemporaneous Christ. It was also a fore-
shadowing of things to come in the Abram (for the shortened
form of Abraham has always been used) of later years. "We
began to meet regularly for prayer and fellowship," he writes.
"We soon got hold of a Bible and began to read the story of
Jesus, and Acts of the Apostles, and the Letters to the Churches.
We grew and got others with us. A man on a neighboring farm
by the name of Gunnar had been putting water in the milk
that he sold and because of a deep conviction of the wrong he
had done, he came to a public confession and restitution for his
misdeeds. He also found forgiveness with God and began to tell
others about it. He opened his home for people of the neighborhood to come to hear the Bible read and to pray. A separate
meeting was arranged for children. I was included. Many
adults were converted. Children and young people were also
added to the happy company to whom God had become a
living reality as a Heavenly Father, and Jesus Christ a living
Saviour.

"Well do I remember that hard-boiled school teacher, how
cruel he was, how little he understood how to help us boys forward. Then one day he came to class with an apology for the
way he had acted, and the attitude he had taken, even while he
was teaching religion. He told us how his eyes had been opened
and that, while he had been as orthodox as the devil, he had
been pharisaical and detached from the Source, out of touch
with the living Christ. But now he had made a personal com-

mitment of himself and received God's gift of pardon, peace and power by receiving Christ. Now there was life and interest in the classes, with a new understanding and glow in his religious instruction. Whether at play or in the classroom he was a new man, whom we all learned to love.

"Father, too, became a new man and our home became a mecca for Christian emissaries and for people of every kind who wanted counsel, fellowship or help.

"Part of my task as a lad was to round up the sheep out in the woods or on the mountain slope during the summer, and bring them to the home farm. I learned to love those sheep and gave them all names. Some seemed wicked and I would climb upon a great boulder and, with the flock of sheep before me, preach to them and warn them of their ways!"

It takes more than youthful enthusiasm, however, to live the Christian life. The walk in the Spirit in which we do not fulfill the lusts of the flesh necessitates the discipline of a regular spiritual diet—the daily reading of the Scriptures and private prayer. Young Abram had to learn this, and the family grew concerned as coldness crept in. "Neglect of my devotional life caused moral defeat," he wrote. But it was not the pointing finger of condemnation that restored him. It was understanding and compassionate love, the faith that still believes that God is at work in the wayward. "My older sisters would warn me; one would scold me for not attending meetings and going to church; but the youngest, Eli, would only follow me with a look of compassion. One day I entered the kitchen where she was alone. Immediately she came toward me and gently pushed me against the door as she put her arms about my neck. Then she looked at me with that deep understanding look and, as tears came to her eyes, she said, 'Abram, have you turned your back on Jesus?' Then as she burst out weeping, with her face on my shoulder, she sank to her knees pulling me down with her. That day she prayed and loved me back to fellowship with God and the family."

2 | THE NEW WORLD

Teen-age years were passing, and the young country lad was approaching manhood. What should it now be? Should he aim high—for college? Should he follow his father on the farm? God had a plan. His ways are not ours. He calls, we follow; but the one necessity is that we are within hearing distance. Abram best tells his own story.

"It was springtime and I was walking behind a plow, when again the sense of God came vividly to me, with the arresting question, 'What are you going to do with your life?' I stopped, meditated, and decided. I knelt in the upturned sod and dedicated my life to full-time service for Him who was nailed to the cross on my behalf and for the redemption of the world.

"The woods, the mountain slopes, the high pinnacles, evenings under the open canopy of heaven with the stars twinkling and the firmament bringing its message of awe-inspiring majesty and glory, scenes from lake and sea, crowd in upon me now with the many memories of the moments such as that, when God spoke and the fellowship with the Unseen became particularly real.

"In addition to public school and private instruction, I had attended a trade school and academy, Ungdomskole, which was a preparation for Prytz College. But in late February of 1905, a young lady from the neighborhood dropped in while we were at the noonday meal. She casually remarked that she had received a ticket from America about a year ago, and now she had been informed that if this ticket was not used within ten days, it would be void, and that she couldn't avail herself of it and didn't know what to do.

"After she had gone, I turned to my Dad and said, 'Father, your finances do not permit me to go on to the university at Oslo, and you believe that I should. In America education is free, money is plentiful, everyone has a chance there. Now here is my opportunity. I can go over there and finish my education, make a pile of money to help you, and return after a few years.'

"Father hesitated and then said, 'Let us ask God about it.' We all bowed in prayer and then after each had had his turn, there was a moment of silence when all turned to Father to speak first, as was the custom. He had tears in his eyes when he said, 'My son, you are my hope and my pride. It is hard to think of you leaving, but I think this is of God.' The four sisters said the same. Then we thanked God and proceeded to make the young fellow ready for his adventure to the new world.

"By the fifth of March he was ready to depart. His new clothes, shoes, a suitcase, a trunk, and everything on his body, were homemade. The clothes were wool from our own sheep, yarn prepared by the sisters, woven and tailored by them. The shoes were the hides of our own sheep and cows. The suitcases and trunk were made by myself; for we had had good training. We had learned to be independent and productive. Work was an honor. The training of the head, the hand and the heart went together.

"The dream of years was about to come true. The longing to see what was behind the mountains and out there in the great world across the sea was about to be realized. The poets like Bjornson, Ibsen and Lie had created the vision, hopes and dreams for accomplishment and attainment. It was a memorable evening when we said goodbye. The old Book had been our daily support and the promises of God there recorded were a mutual comfort at that time.

"From the deck of the steamer it was not only a waving goodbye to loved ones, but to the hills, woods and mountains, and the beautiful sea lying peaceful, deep and unsearchable as the human heart. The Scripture verse that came to me was from Isaiah 54:10: 'For the mountains shall depart and the hills be removed, but my kindness shall not depart from thee, neither shall the covenant of my peace be removed, saith the Lord that hath mercy on thee.'

"What a conglomeration of human beings from various parts of Europe and the Near East crowded aboard the White Star liner at Liverpool a few days later! Special barracks were built in the storage part of the ship to accommodate many of us third class passengers. It was a stormy voyage. Men who started out in profanity, vulgarity and pride, later were found praying and crying out to God to stay the elements and give succor and safety. A few Swedish emigrants were singing, 'Tryggare kan ingen vara enn Guds lilla barnaskara' (Safer can nobody be than God's own little flock)."

The first sight of America was a thrilling experience. Like a good Norwegian, he saw everything through Norwegian eyes. "We recalled," he wrote, "that the Norsemen discovered this country about the year 1000 and left their marks behind in Rhode Island. We recalled how this fact was recorded at the Vatican, where a cousin of Christopher Columbus worked and from where he received the information he needed, which gave him the added confirmation to support him in his venture which resulted in the rediscovery of America in 1492. We recalled the adventure of the Norsemen in pioneering this country, in clearing the forests, opening the mines, cultivating the fields, developing the fishing industry and arriving at positions of leadership in various fields of endeavor, education, government and the professions, and how this land had become a haven of refuge for people from all countries."

Landing at Ellis Island, a little incident took place which did more than anything else to seal to young Abram's heart that he had come to the place of God's choice for his life. "We were greeted," he continued, "by a woman with a radiant face who handed me a copy of the New Testament, making this comment: 'Welcome to America. Here is the Book upon which this country was founded, the secret of our greatness, prosperity and strength. May this be a light upon your pathway and a lamp unto your feet. It is God's message to men.'" "Since then," Abram added, "I have always carried a New Testament in my pocket and read it every day."

"So this is America!" he commented. "My, what a rush there is everywhere! Everybody seems to be in a hurry. What a contrast to the old country!"

3 | SHOCKS

Fifteen days travel took Abram westward through "stretches of land, over mountains, through valleys and endless expanses of prairies," to what was then the rough, tough frontier town of Butte, Montana. Of those experiences he wrote:

"The sheltered life and balmy spiritual atmosphere of home and community were left behind. The emigration promoters sent abroad to recruit settlers for the great prairies, told fanciful stories about the superabundance of gold, grub, game and gaiety in the New World. But the month of March in 1905 in Butte, Montana, presented a different story so far as this immigrant was concerned.

"The man whose address I had, lived in a shack by the railroad track. His associates had similar abodes. They were given to drink, women and gambling. 'Well, come, young fellow,' said A.B., who had provided a few blankets in the adjoining shed for my accommodation, 'let's go up town and meet the boys. We'll make an American out of you in a hurry.'

"He escorted me through the red light district, at the corner of which there was a large saloon, with a strange mingling of men and women of an appearance and behavior that was entirely foreign to me. In the fashion of typical western hospitality he shouted to the gang to line up to be introduced to the newcomer and initiate him in American society.

"Behind the long bar along the wall were large mirrors and bottles of every description. Moving back and forth were heavy-set men, bleary-eyed, with swollen cheeks and overdeveloped fronts. Glasses were filled and with a 'Welcome' and 'Good luck in America,' they lifted their glasses for a toast to the newcomer.

"It would have been socially proper for me to have responded, but I left my glass untouched, and then coaxing and cursing began. 'You are away from mother's skirts—now be a man. Act like a man—drink. You are in America now—do like Americans do. Come on, don't be a sissy. Have a drink.'

" 'No, thank you. I never tasted liquor in my life and I can get along without it.' There was a power beyond myself that strengthened me to say 'no,' and courteously to thank my host and excuse myself.

"It was a cold, clear night and I walked out into the strange city with a life so foreign, and so rude and crude. I walked and walked up onto the jagged cliffs of the Rockies which form a background to the city.

"There in a sheltered nook overlooking the city and the valley below, I looked from the glittering lights of the mines and homes to the beautiful dome of the firmament above. Below things were so strange, so full of foreboding of evil days, but looking up I recognized the same stars as shone over Norway, that spoke their mysterious language and made their impression on my boyish mind and soul.

"It was easy to weep and long for home. It was easy to pray. That night God met me afresh with reassurance and comfort. A verse from the Book of Proverbs became significant, stating that 'there is yet a future and your hope shall not come to naught.' It was with determined steps and resolute commitment to know and do God's will, to trust and obey Him, that I went back to my humble abode in the railroad section of this mining town of some 60,000 population.

"Tramp, tramp, tramp, from morning till night, looking for a job. Each day was an introduction to a little different phase of life in this frontier of the American melting pot. Each day was a chance to mingle with others who found life hard and had a tough situation to face. Finally a cursing Irishman gave me a chance as a section hand at $1.75 a day.

"The hard labor and the copper-tinged water put me out of commission after two weeks. I don't recall how long I was laid up in that shack, as part of the time I was unconscious. But this I recall, that it was again an opportunity of discovering God, who gives comfort and manifests Himself according to our needs. The European starch had to be washed out and the attitude of my national superiority had to be eliminated by learning to discover the gold in men of every class, race or creed, as well as to see in clear manifestation the awful wickedness of all men without God, regardless of background, when the restraint of convention is withdrawn. The trials and testings that followed represented the best schooling that I could have.

"Three times I was beaten out of my wages, cursed as a big-footed Norwegian or a darn Swede. The Fourth of July was the last straw. I had a job as painter in a mountain village. I worked hard and on the Fourth morning asked for my pay, in order to buy some American clothes and go out with the others to celebrate. Denied that, and having only a dollar, when I heard the train whistle, bound from Basin to Butte, I said good-bye, took my little bundle, secured my ticket for Butte at ninety cents, and with ten cents in my pocket landed in that city with the big question—Now what?

"For ten cents you could get a glass of milk and two rolls. The cry of my stomach was for food, but the cry of my heart was for God. For ten cents I could get a streetcar to the outskirts of the city, Columbia Gardens, and find a nook among the trees and be alone. I went. There in the furthest corner, away from the celebrating crowds, I was buried with my griefs, loneliness and tears. God and men had forsaken me. I wanted to die. If God really loved me and cared, why wouldn't He help me? It was too far back to the city to walk, I had no food, no place to sleep, no friends, and no money.

"I took out my Testament and read, 'Ye have not chosen me, but I chose you and appointed you that you should go forth and bear fruit and that the fruit should remain, that whatsoever you ask the Father in my name, he shall give it you. This I command you, to love one another. If the world hates you, you know it has hated me before it hated you. If you were of the world, the world would love its own, but because you are not of the world, but I chose you out of the world, therefore the world hates you. Remember the word that I said to you. A servant is not greater than his master. They persecuted me, they will persecute you. If they kept my word, they will keep yours also. But all this they will do to you because they do not know him who sent me.' And, 'fear not, for I am with you. In the world you have tribulation, but be of good cheer, I have overcome the world.'

"I wiped away my tears and looked up and thanked God. A deep sense of security and joy possessed me. I belonged to Him and it was His business to look after me.

"'My, what does he want?' I said to myself, seeing a large man with brown face coming up between the trees. As he discovered me, he spoke. When I answered, he detected my accent and asked if I were a Norwegian. I answered in the affirmative. He noticed the New Testament in my hand and asked if I were a Christian. Again an affirmative answer. And then he rushed toward me, put out his big, strong arms and gave me an embrace with fatherly tenderness, saying, 'I, too, am a Christian and of Norwegian birth. How in the world is it that you are here?"

"I told him briefly my story and then he told me his—how he, too, had been introduced to the American saloon and brought from the abyss of iniquity. But while working as a bartender, somebody had pitched a tent in an empty lot next door. There the preaching and singing aroused the interest of his customers and caused many of them to be converted, and one night he had been back of the saloon listening, till he, too, had been convicted of his evil ways and lost condition. At the conclusion of the meeting in the tent he had sought out the preacher, who subsequently had come to the back of the saloon to pray with him and point him to the sinner's only hope, Jesus. Now he was working in a copper mine on the 2800 level where, at every four-hour shift, men would come to him for prayer and counsel, and to learn how he had experienced God's power to restore and keep.

" 'By the way,' said he, 'come on down. My family is here. We drove out with our horse and buggy and brought a picnic dinner along, my wife and two daughters and my son.'

"That day I wrote my declaration of independence. A new chapter began. That was my first introduction to an American family, to homemade food, to Christian American hospitality, and through them to church and to a colony of men and women who had heaven in their hearts. While they worked and lived among the sordid associations in a wicked city, their homes were clean, and wherever there was a little patch of ground, there would be a flower or little tree planted. They created a new environment and produced evidence of the fact that Jesus Christ lived.

"Sunday they brought me to church. There was no church of my own denomination, the Lutheran, and I was scared stiff to enter any other, particularly the Methodist Church to which they brought me. I was literally afraid that God would slay me for doing such a wicked thing. I really believed that the only church was my church, everybody else was wrong and damned. It was with fear and trembling that I sat in the back seat.

"To my great surprise, the hearty singing was of hymns I knew from home. The language was a mixture of Norwegian and Danish, the spirit was fervent. There was a glow of reality, joy and freedom. The preaching was an exposition of a Bible story and from the heart and experience.

"At the conclusion of the service, the tall, sturdy preacher was at the door shaking hands with all the people as they went out. I was dumbfounded when he asked me to come downstairs and have dinner with him and his family. That proved to be a risky business, for I accepted the invitation and fell in love with his oldest daughter. Of course, to start with, it was just an attraction. She was cordial to me. I noticed she was competent in the kitchen and in serving at the table. She was a good singer, she could handle the piano very well, and the mandolin, violin and guitar. But, of course, I was just an immigrant and she a minister's daughter, so I couldn't think about anything along the lines of a love affair.

"But her three brothers also took an interest in me, and the people of the little church were all so friendly and helpful. They found me a job and I began to feel adjusted. One job was at Peterson's boarding house as a substitute, working from 3:30 in the moring till 8:00 at night, with two hours' rest in the forenoon and two in the afternoon. This was peeling potatoes, cleaning out the spitoons and the washroom, and preparing things for the kitchen.

"My basement bedroom had no light from the outside, but it furnished me much light on the inside for heart and mind, for here I read through much of my Bible on my knees. This made me immune to the horrible temptations that I daily confronted from wicked women and bad men.

"Young people, living on a higher level, with the church as their social and inspirational center, gave me the fellowship needed. Other immigrants from the Scandinavian countries who also had to face the problems of life, began to find the same solution and fellowship. Teamwork for temperance, social decency, economic adjustment and spiritual reality became a happy experience during the rest of my stay in that city.

"Then the preacher moved to Kalispell, Montana, and with him his large family, save the two eldest boys, who were employed in Butte. I became interested in the possibility of a job in the same town. There was a certain social attraction also.

"The early summer of the next year found me in this charming valley of northwestern Montana, west of the Rocky Mountains, near the beautiful Flathead Lake. A job was waiting for me in the sawmill. The preacher greeted me cordially and put me to work.

"Life with the lumberjacks was again an education. Fellowship with wholesome farmers of the valley and workers in the small town, and life in a more settled, stable community, was a happy contrast to the turbulent life in Butte. The preacher's eldest daughter was the organist, the choir director, the leader of a string band and the vibrant leader among the young people. This girl became increasing good company, although she didn't evidence much interest in me.

"The preacher, the Rev. N. L. Hansen, a Dane, was one of the oldtime Methodist pioneers traveling from place to place holding camp meetings, visiting the homesteaders in their primitive adobe dwellings. These rugged men, without assured stipend and often without a manse, knew that life of sacrifice for the Gospel's sake which is the backbone of a militant church. He had now become Superintendent for the Rocky Mountain district. He seemed to see in me certain possibilities and had given me a course of training and then a preacher's license. This made it possible for him to give me an appointment as missionary and pastor.

"They had a birthday party for me on Sunday, October 7, 1906. I was twenty years old. That evening I was sent to take charge of a missionary territory with headquarters at Great Falls, Montana.

"When I came to the little white parsonage next to the church, the president of the Board of Trustees looked at me in silence, measured me with his eyes from head to foot and then finally exclaimed, 'Say, you're nothing but a kid, but we'll try you out.' My salary was fifty dollars a month. I had to get furnishings for the house, and a bicycle. Saddle horses could be borrowed in the different sections of the surrounding territory.

"At the altar of that little church the angels from glory witnessed much prayer and many tears. First from the preacher, second from the immigrants who needed God. Most Sundays were given to the services in this church, and the week was devoted to traveling around in a radius of seventy miles, from the Rockies in the west and the Highwood Mountains to the east, to the settlements where there were no public schools and where the ministry included being teacher, preacher, doctor and social worker. Some sections were reached by bicycle, and others by train or horseback.

"It was a thrilling experience over those rolling prairies and mountains, with cowboys, Indians and pioneers of every kind. In a coonskin coat, sheepskin pants, cowboy hat and a broncho horse, with a revolver on one side and a Bible on the other, I sought to be a friend to saint and sinner, to rich and poor, to men of every description, seeking to represent Him who came not to be ministered unto, but to minister, and to give His life a ransom for many."

4 | THE PRAIRIE PREACHER

"Great Falls, by the mighty Missouri River and the wind-swept plains and bare hills, was also the scene of many spiritual battles," he continued. "It was here that I first discovered God's provision to meet my hunger for the fullness of the Holy Spirit, first as an epochal experience by full surrender—our all for His all—and then as an expanding life through faith. My own inadequacy made it necessary for me to seek and to cry out for God's adequacy. His Word and His Spirit, through faith and obedience, flooded my being with love and joy, and gave me victory in the work. I could love people I didn't like.

"It was here, too, that I began to learn to pray for the sick. One instance stands out. I was called to the hospital where I found the doctors and the nurses by the bedside of a prominent young woman. They informed me she had but a short time to live and that she was afraid to die. 'Will you prepare her to go,' said one of the doctors. I gave her the message from Jesus the Christ and knelt by her side in prayer. As God gave her grace to believe His word and accept the Lord Jesus Christ for salvation and eternal life, I was led by His Spirit to pray for her healing and to claim it. The touch of God came upon her to the utter astonishment of all—including myself. The next day she was dismissed from the hospital healed. Many evidences of God's power to heal in answer to prayer and faith have been witnessed since.

"One week I was particularly hard-pressed in finance. Twenty-five dollars had to be paid on Monday. Every nickel had to be watched. The meals were sparse and I didn't have the money to meet my obligation. Sunday afternoon I went to the church to pray. I committed myself and my problem to God, and left it there.

"At the conclusion of the evening service, I was saying good-bye to the people when a middle-aged woman whom I scarcely knew pressed a paper into my hand. I put it in my pocket without looking. A number of people had lingered and had come to the altar for prayer. I thought possibly that this note was a request for prayer, so I pulled it out to see. There I found twenty-five dollars. I thanked God and took courage.

"The next day I had difficulty in locating this woman, first to learn her name and secondly her address. When I came to her house, she was evidently embarassed, and then I told her my story, my need and my prayer. She then related how on Sunday afternoon she was so forcibly impressed to give me some money. She went and pulled out five dollars to take along to church; but she didn't get any peace about that and got another five, and then ten; but she got no rest until, in obedience to the inner voice, she pulled out another five dollars. This was big money in those days, but when she had taken that twenty-five dollars and put it in her purse to take along to give me, great peace filled her heart. She further related that when she had given me the money that Sunday night, she went home walking on air, she felt so happy and rich. She recognized that she had been God's messenger.

"Far to the northwest, close by the Rockies, was a settlement pioneered by a man who persuaded neighbors from his community in Wisconsin to get away from there because of a spiritual revival that was making people 'fanatics.' They had settled thirty-two miles from the railroad to become isolated from any religious influence and build a community of their own choice. When I landed there one wintry night and found lodging with two bachelors, I told them that I would like to meet with the people and tell them the good news of the good Book.

They became curious and helpful. A long general ring on the improvised telephone service, utilizing the fence wire, brought everybody to the telephone. He told them a youngster from Norway had arrived who had a story to tell and that he would be at the community loghouse that evening at eight o'clock.

"The place was packed. I told my story and asked the people to give God a chance in their lives, without whom life was a minus, and with whom life is a plus, and that Jesus Christ had come, inviting us to accept Him and what He had to offer. It was a simple story by a simple boy, who sought to be true to his calling. One whole family responded that night and remained after the meeting. They prevailed on me to go home with them. That home became my home every time I visited that section. For warm woolen socks, good food, good fellowship and a good broncho horse to ride, that was the place! The man who ran away from God in Wisconsin found God in that community and later with his family became effective transmitters of the new life to many others in the Swan River Valley.

"A summer conference in 1908 brought many friends together from Kalispell and surrounding territory to the head of Flathead Lake. The District Superintendent was in charge. Several ministers were there; but the center of attraction was the Superintendent's daughter, who had moved with him from La Crosse, Wisconsin, to Utah and Spokane, Kalispell, Great Falls, Butte, and now back to Kalispell again.

"An inner compulsion made me ask her for a walk after the meeting the last night. On the top of the hill, at the edge of the lake, overlooking the vast panorama of valleys and wood-covered hills, the snow-covered Rockies to the east, the silvery lake, the fleecy clouds and the moonlit heavens and earth, I turned to a good, pure woman and told her that I loved her and asked her to be my wife. After some hesitation, Mattie Hansen haltingly acquiesced and we knelt down to pray."

5 | WEDDED--TO WIFE AND COUNTRY

Two years of preparation for the Methodist ministry followed at Evanston, Illinois. Studies were doubled up by enrollment in four departments consecutively, the Norwegian-Danish Theological Seminary, the Garratt Biblical, the Academy, and the Northwestern University College of Liberal Arts. In facing the severe onslaught of radical schools of Biblical criticism, a word of a Swedish nurse was a stand-by: "Don't forget to let your dedication keep pace with your education." At the same time Abram found on the faculties "great personalities, towering men of God, with humility and power among men in the pulpit, and giving much helpful material to students in the various classes."

He had a student appointment at Kenosha, Wisconsin, and there fought and won his first battle with severe division in a church. "Progress seemed impossible," he records. "There were many fine people, especially among the youngsters, but the church was divided into two groups, and two of the elders in the church were the dividing factors.

"Every Friday night we met for a period of Bible study, prayer and testimonies. I had prayed much one afternoon that God would convict and give victory, or I must quit. After a brief message that night, we bowed in prayer. After a while I heard a low rumbling, and I looked up and saw the most important man in the congregation, a stubborn, self-willed, keen and able executive, who was superintendent of the Sunday school and president of the Board of Trustees, walk over to the other side and whisper to a nearly equally capable elder of the church, and then they both knelt down and began to weep and pray. There had been a reconciliation, each had asked the other for forgiveness, and they both asked God to forgive and to make them what they should be.

"When that happened, it electrified the rest. Within a few weeks thirty-seven of the young people had come to open acknowledgment of Christ and into a fervent Christian experience. It was heavenly to work in their midst."

But before two years had passed in that stimulating environment of school and church, students and community, the unexpected happened. "One day," he said, "one of my professors preached my funeral sermon to the student body, saying that Vereide had to go west with tuberculosis, and that the doctor did not entertain much hope." Though this ended his college career, in the surprisingly short time of three months "under

31

Abram and Mattie Vereide were married in 1910.

God's cure of Montana's ozone, pine air, codliver oil and adequate rest," he was well enough to go into the insurance business during the week and occasionally speak on Sundays; and to look forward again to a life of full vigor.

With the doctor declaring him cured, in August of 1910, the wedding bells were ringing, and "at the altar of the little church of happy memories in Kalispell," he records, "the preacher's daughter whom I first saw in Butte, knelt with me and joined hands to receive the blessing of God as husband and wife. Her father performed the ceremony."

The first assignment of their married life was Spokane, Washington. "It was a humming center of American life in this capital of the Inland Empire," he continues. "Immigrants would come for employment, and we became an employment agency. They would come to learn English, and we established English and Americanization classes. They would come for counsel and help, and we became an adjustment clinic. They would come to meet each other, and it became a social center. They would come to sing, to study, to pray, to worship. Rarely would we have a meal by ourselves. Human need was constantly before us. What we had we shared with others. We were young and strong, full of life and interest, reaching out to surrounding centers and to the various aspects of life in the city.

"What a joy to be alive and live for others, constantly seeing people moving from groping to certainty, defeat to victory, death to life, from self-centeredness to Christ-centeredness, a procession of people moving on to the arena of usefulness, as assets to the community and the country of their choice!

"The unexpected again happened when I was invited back to Great Falls for some meetings. In the audience was a successful business man who had been a saloon-keeper, but whom together with that marvelous Montana Pioneer, W. W. Van Orsdel, I had been privileged to lead into the Christian life, as well as his wife. He requested to see me after the meeting. He asked if I didn't want to go back to Norway to see my father. 'Of course,' said I, 'I'd like to go, but it is out of the question, as you know, because of finances.' 'Well,' he replied, 'that is not the question. If you can adjust your affairs so that you can go, I will take care of the expenses. You led me to Christ and made possible a happy home and a useful and successful life. The least I can do is to provide that for you.'

"I accepted, and that summer in Norway I discoverd that I was an American! It came about in this way. After the indescribable joy of being with my father and sisters, friends and relatives, I was invited to speak at various points on the northwest coast, and among these in a place where one of my sisters was a teacher.

"On a beautiful night, towards the midnight sun, when preparing to board the steamer, somebody called out in ringing English from the upper deck, 'Well, well, isn't it Mr. Vereide from Spokane?' Then he waved the American flag.

"Something burst within me. I hurriedly climbed the ladder on the side of the ship and found my way to this friend from America. I grabbed the flag and waved it and kissed it; it was my flag. I greeted these friends as relatives, and feasted on nothing but English that whole night. I discovered I was an American.

"While my citizenship papers had been obtained some time before, up to that time my gaze had been backward to the Old World, and the emphasis had been on the first part of the hyphenated word, Norwegian-American. Now like a glorious burst of sunshine, it overwhelmed me in a sudden flash of glory—the wonder of the fact that I was an American, from within out."

In later years, the love of his adopted country, implanted at this time and deepening through the years, was to be used by God to embolden him to challenge its lawmakers on city, state, and federal levels with the necessity of a "leadership led by God." Often at Rotary or Kiwanis luncheons he would tell of another occasion when returning from a trip abroad, as they approached New York, "visibility was limited to the length of the ship. Standing on the upper deck, with anticipation, a never-to-be-forgotten sight burst on me. There was a rift in the clouds, and before us loomed up the Statue of Liberty bathed in the glowing sun, with the torch of freedom pointing high, land of the unchained Bible, home for the teeming millions, beckoning us to its doors of opportunity and to fellowship with free men in a free world. I wept and cried out, 'Oh, land of the free, the home of the brave, you are mine, you are mine!' "

On the return from this first trip, "it was with eager anticipation that I set foot again on American soil," he continued, "tramping the ground with firm foot as I landed, getting hold of some good soil, squeezing it in my hands with a sense of ownership, and breathing the free air among free men; for I was privileged to be one of them in the building and making of the America of our dreams.

"It was on the beautiful height above the city of Astoria, Oregon, where I came for the annual conference that year, that I stood in solemn meditation, reflecting upon the recent experiences in Europe, my eight years in the U.S.A., the America that had been, was and what it might become, and rededicated my life to that place and part which God in His purpose would want me to take; and that I, with brain and brawn and heart, might be God's maximum for His kingdom and the country and people for whom I was privileged to live and work."

6 | MAN WHO WON'T TAKE "NO"

Portland, Oregon was the next move, a considerable promotion to a new church and parsonage, the most coveted in the conference. The early days of pioneering on horseback with Bible in one pocket and gun in another had been an ideal training ground in hard living and human relationships. But the outline of God's real plan for this young life was now coming into view, not in the saddle in lonely places, but in the teeming life of the city; not, it was soon to be seen, among those who have had the bottom knocked out of life, its derelicts, its failures, nor even in the mainstream of average humanity with their daily pressures and problems; but, ultimately, among those even more in need, who live dangerously in high places, where the strong winds of success and fame and great responsibilities blow tempestuously, where the horizon is limitless and the air invigorating, but the climbing arduous and falls precipitous.

God has His specialists. The unique and distinctive calling for which God was fitting Abram was still some years ahead.

Alicia Vereide Abrahamsen.

These were still preparatory years. We might call them a second phase. The first early years had been the training of God's worker. These next years are the development of the worker in the work. They lead on to the ultimate commission in which Abram "serves his own generation in the will of God . . . a vessel meet for the Master's use, prepared unto every good work."

The three years in this downtown church in Portland were filled with activity spiritual and social, with their own little family growing up around them, their one daughter, Alicia, born in Spokane, a son, Warren, born in Portland, and two more sons, Milton and Abraham (Abe) in later years.

Two incidents stand out in these years. One was the lesson in prevailing prayer from an old couple who had an only child, who specialized in fishing salmon in the Columbia River. He had become a hopeless drunkard. "One day," said Abram, "his frail mother informed me that she was going to remain in her house in prayer and fasting until her son was converted. That evening I was addressing a congregation in another section of the city. As I stepped off the streetcar that night, I saw this man stumbling along, endeavoring to keep within the limits of the sidewalk. I was silently praying that he would not come to the church and disturb the meeting. Later, I discovered he was there and well to the front. I had barely got started with my message when this fellow came forward and knelt at the altar, sobbing and praying. A young lady of culture and refinement, who had known him since his childhood, came immediately forward and knelt at his side to pray for him. That evening he became a transformed individual. Upon his return home, he found his mother and father praising God, for they had the victory already. They had received full assurance from God through the prayer of faith."

The other incident was typical of the boldness which was to become such a characteristic of Abram's later ministry. "We had $500 left on the church debt," he recalls. "It had to be paid off before other improvements and advances could be thought of. During my morning meditation one day, the thought came to me that the famous Billy Sunday, who was summering on his fruit ranch some sixty miles away, should be secured to address a meeting and we would charge admission. By this means two ends could be gained, the money to pay off the debt and a spiritual blessing to the community. My official board demurred. They did not think it could be done, and they did not want to make the investment, even as small as that, of going out to see him, believing it would be futile. I met their objection by saying that I would pay my own expenses if I didn't get him; but if I did, they would be taken care of from the proceeds of the meeting. To this they agreed.

"At Hood River the mailman informed me that Billy Sunday received somewhere around 1000 letters a day, and that practically every day delegations came there to see him, but he turned them all down. My heart sank within me, but I prayed some more and received courage to go on, hiring a rig to drive through the valley to his farm. Ma Sunday, his wife, took care of the interviews with any visitors. I noticed she was already engaged with some of these, and others were waiting. I soon realized there was no chance through that channel. Wandering through the orchard, I discovered a bareheaded man at work among the trees. I recognized the face of the famous Billy Sunday. I approached him with a 'How do you do, Mr. Sunday,' but he didn't recognize me or answer me. I repeated my greeting and came closer, but he proceeded to go away from me without regarding my salutation. I spoke louder and came closer, and then he grunted back, 'What do you want?' Said I, 'I want to see you.' Said he, 'I am not here to see people,' and went his way. But I followed close after him and continued to tell my story—that I was pastor of a Norwegian-Danish church, seeking to win immigrants for Christian citizenship and useful careers. I told him about the problem of the church debt and my hopes and plans. He turned about, looked at me and said, 'Well, I had a Norwegian sweetheart once.' This opened a conversation, which resulted in his coming to Portland without any charge and as my guest.

"The largest church in the city was packed to overflowing. Billy delivered a great sermon, at the conclusion of which many accepted Christ as their Savior and backsliders were restored. The $500 debt was paid from the proceeds of the evening and some money left over, after the traveling expenses and incidentals in connection with getting him there were taken care of. At a very exclusive luncheon for the upper two hundred of Portland in the Diamond Room of the Benson Hotel Billy Sunday gave one of the most magnificent addresses I have ever heard. The president of the Southern Pacific Railway introduced him with the words, 'Ladies and gentlemen,' then turning round to Billy Sunday, pointed his finger, 'Billy, fire . . .' Off went that orator, famous for his slang; but on this occasion he used the choicest English and drew his lessons from history, from literature, from science, from experience, and from the Bible, concluding with the statement 'Men, you must be Christians, little children will love you, pure women will admire you, men will respect you, and God Almighty will crown your life at last with His glory.' That sophisticated audience rose to their feet, waved their handkerchiefs, many wiped their tears, with handclaps and a great ovation. That was Billy Sunday in a setting in which I had never seen or heard him before."

Appointment as District Superintendent for the Northwest took Abram on a visit to Alaska and to a work which greatly impressed him, that of Father Duncan on the Metliketla Island where "an Indian cannibal tribe had been converted and the only real Christian civilization established under the Stars and Stripes." Such an effect of spiritual transformation on civic and social conditions was exactly what he felt so strongly should be a normal product of Christianity, which "isn't only a doctrine, but a life." However, it would be right to note, to keep the truth in perspective, that problems and disappointments in the Metliketla Island in later years underline the fact that the kingdom of God in its complete external form will never be realized in this unredeemed world until Christ returns in person and "Satan is bound," as the New Testament Scriptures make very clear. Any attempt to set up such a kingdom has always ended in failure, and always will, whether in the larger concept of Augustine's famed "City of God," or the Holy Roman Empire, or in lesser localized communities. The impression that Father Duncan's work made on Abram does not mean that he had any groundlessly idealistic ideas of a Christian Utopia. His journals have many references to the "glorious hope of the Church," the return of its Head in person; but a vital part of the message God has given him is to challenge all professing Christians with their obligations to be God-led and Christ-centered in their business, social and civic responsibilities, and that those in leadership in the nations should themselves be led by God in their far-reaching decisions and in their public statements, as well as in their personal lives.

7 | SEVEN DYNAMIC YEARS

In 1916 Abram moved from Portland to Seattle, having been appointed to the most strategic church in the whole conference. There followed the most dynamic seven years of his ministry as pastoral, evangelistic and social worker.

"We gloried in the pulsating life of a metropolitan center," Abram writes, "the gateway to Alaska, to the Orient, a capital for the fishing industry, among whom were so many from our homeland, a great center for logging and lumbering, shipping, shipbuilding, various minor industries, educational institutions, and a terminal of transcontinental railroads.

"Our home was a mecca for the people we were there to serve. We found it needful to establish a home for girls, immigrants largely, a home for men, a home for delinquents, the Ruth School, an employment office, Americanization classes, Bible classes and various other classes of instruction. And then the joy of a crowded church with definite, visible spiritual results each week. Life was full and rich. We lived by the side of the road and were friends to man. There were many neglected communities without church or Sunday school in that area. My missionary zeal drove me out on Sunday afternoons or some week day, visiting among the people in some section, and having public meetings in home, hall or school house."

This vigorous combination of a soul-saving work with care for the bodies and minds of those in need caused the City Union of Seattle to elect him to head up an enterprise which combined industrial relief with the training of the handicapped and Christian social service. Mr. R. E. Stewart furnished the funds for three months of research throughout the country in this field. Clint W. Lee, O. T. Oliver, C. F. Greiner, R. E. Stewart and C. Winant were "choice men" as directors of this community enterprise, which was so urgent in those years of the great depression, with the unemployed numbering millions. To Abram, the venture was a "coveted opportunity." On his return, based on his report, it was decided to form a non-denominational corporation called Good Will Industries.

Alicia, their daughter, remembers how her mother washed and ironed for the children at night, so as to take care of homeless men and women for whom they made a home in the church, while they won them for the Lord, taught them citizenship and got them jobs. During the day time she would teach them to cook and do household duties. "They always had some drunks sleeping on the front porch, whom they would pick off the street, get sober, and then would go and see their families. I remember stepping over them at night to get into the house. Dad was always for the whole man—a good citizen is to be a good Christian, the two woven together in the fibre of the country." As Abram put it, "The passion of my life at that time was to win immigrants for Christ and help them to become real assets as industrious and patriotic citizens. I insisted that there must be a dedicated heart, a dedicated head, and a dedicated hand. A symmetrical development was essential. From Alaska to California you will find many faithful citizens of integrity and worth, who date their beginning in a successful life in the New World to meetings or personal interviews at the church or parsonage at Boren Avenue and Stewart Street in Seattle, Washington. There the decision was made and they discovered for themselves the truth of the statement recorded in John 1:12: 'To as many as received him, to them gave he power to become the sons of God, even to them that believe on his name, which were born, not of the will of the flesh, nor of the will of man, but of God.' There is nothing to be compared to the joy of leading people to Christ and into a Christian experience. There is nothing more important and far-reaching for the individual and society. In Daniel 12 we read: 'And they that be wise shall shine as the brightness of the firmament, and they that turn many to righteousness as the stars for ever and ever.' 'He that winneth souls is wise.'

"When I was in Norway in 1946, a man whom I hadn't seen or heard from for many years, wrote me telling me about

41

his success in Norway, the prosperity and progress that had been made, the happy home life and his Christian family, and his place and part in the community and church. Then he concluded by saying, 'All this dates back to those early days in Seattle, where you led me to a personal acceptance of Jesus Christ as my Saviour and my Lord, and helped me to become established as a Christian in my new environment.' "

Vereide often used to speak on the close connection between the Norsemen and the New World, and was in demand as a lecturer on this subject. "We have roots in the old soil," he said, "which feed on new life in our adopted country, but the complete separation from the old would be detrimental to the individual life as well as the social order." He would speak as a Norwegian of their history reaching back to the beginning of the Christian era, of the wonderful literature, and of the great national experiences that served to mold the nation. "We remember the victories of the Vikings in Constantinople, France and England. We have the remarkable collection of prose and poetry in 'the Older and Younger Edda' from the earliest times. As children we learned to think with a Bjornstjerne Bjornson, Henrik Wergeland, Jonas Lie, Arne Garborg, H. C. Andersen, and Henrik Ibsen. Ole Bull and Edvard Grieg gave us music; Gude, Tideman and Sinding gave us the great paintings; Bugge was our great historian; Nansen and Amundsen our explorers; and in George Brandes we have the greatest literary critic."

He would then proceed to recount various connecting links between Norway and the New World. The discovery of America was due to a Norseman. "Eric the Red accepted Christianity and in real apostolic zeal went to Greenland with the message of Christ. Later, his son, Leif Ericsson, with a choice company, set out on the same mission; but during a severe storm they lost their way, and after a perilous journey landed in a new country which they called Vineland—Nova Scotia. The first white baby born on American soil was Snorre Sturlason, born 1003, who became the great historian. As was the custom, events of interest were brought to the Pope and reported at the Vatican. Christopher Columbus visited the Eternal City, where a cousin of his was working, and there obtained the desired information about the discovery by

Norsemen of land in the far west. This among other things gave the impetus to Columbus for his famous journey in 1492.

"The Father of this country was a Norseman. According to McCalls' *History of Scandinavians in Pennsylvania,* we read that George Washington was present at a meeting of a society in New York which called itself Scandinavia. George Washington, as a general, was decorating a soldier, and in his speech he said he was very pleased to be with his kinfolks, because his forebears on his father's side emigrated from Denmark in 970, where they lived on a large estate called Wass. From here they came to Derhamshire, England, where they built another estate called after their homestead in Denmark— Wassinga-tune (town of Wass)."

He would continue to trace the great part Scandinavians have had in the birth and development of the U.S.A. The fifteenth Wisconsin Regiment, with 4,500 Norwegians, was a great factor in the victory of the Civil War. The Norwegians of Wisconsin also had a decisive share in Abraham Lincoln becoming president. The results of the election seemed likely to be a draw until the report came from the large community of Norwegians in Wisconsin who were all opposed to slavery and had voted solidly for Lincoln. This decided the election. Many of those who "pierced the wilderness and opened the way to civilization in the west" were Norse pioneers. Kleng Person from Stavanger, Norway, first entered the interior of America and brought settlers with him to Fox Hill, Illinois, and then to Iowa. "Is it not the Scandinavians who have pioneered the way across the plains of Minnesota, the Dakotas, Montana, Idaho, and out in the great northwest? Who had the courage to clear the stump land of Washington? A good majority of them were Scandinavians."

Due to the fact that there was an overlapping in the field of social agencies in the state of Washington and lack of co-ordination and understanding of each other's function, the State Conference of Social Work was organized, and a Social Directory issued. Forty-nine thousand housewives were enlisted and thirty-seven chapters of these women formed to cooperate in turning "waste into wages and junk into jobs," thus producing employment and constructive social service. Miss E. A. Southmayd was the secretary, Mrs. Gertrude

Brawley and Mrs. N. Frayn, president and vice-president of the Women's Auxiliary.

Shops, stores, and industry joined with these housewives in setting aside discarded goods, which were collected at this central place for sorting, distribution, remaking, and resale, or for the making of new articles. This in turn was disposed of from eleven different stores to needy people who could not afford to buy new goods. Several hundred people, who otherwise would be dependent on the taxpayers or the contributing public for their support, were given employment, paid wages, trained, rehabilitated, and as far as possible led into a Christian life.

For two years Abram combined the work of the church and the Good Will Industries, until the load became too heavy and the church appointed assistant ministers. But both the experience in organization and the greatly enlarged insight into conditions in the national life, and widening contacts with men of affairs were the next stages in the development of God's plan for him. Handling the city's organization for the relief of civic distress laid the foundation for handling the city's greater problems of civic redemption from the clutches of subversive elements.

The work grew to the extent that they had to have a building of their own. They started by prayer that God would give a token of His will. It came when Abram returned to his office one day and found there a check for $1000 from a man he scarcely knew, and to whom no mention had been made of their need and hopes. Ultimately the sum reached $67,000, and the building now occupies a whole block in the city.

One unforgettable interview took place one day. "Going past the employment office," writes Abram, "I saw in that long line of men waiting to be interviewed a face that I had seen before, but I could not place him. I observed that he was a wretched piece of humanity, his shoes largely gone, trousers torn, coat dirty, shirt open, and his face unshaven. He bore the marks of a wasted life. Who was he?

"From my office I telephoned to the employment manager, Mr. C. P. Culver, describing the fellow, and requested that he expedite his case and then telephone me about him and send him to my office.

"When he came in, I asked him about his mother and family, and then looked him intently in the face and said, 'Halfdan, do you remember a certain night in the month of March, 1905, at the bar of a saloon in Butte, Montana, where you took particular pains in ridiculing and cursing a certain newcomer because he wouldn't drink, and sneered at him with an oath because he left the party and went out of doors?'

"The fellow got scared and was about to leave, but I locked the door and said to him, 'Halfdan, I know your mother and father, your sister and brothers. In answer to their prayers you have been sent to me today. I am here now to help you back to decency and a future. I don't need to remind you about your need and that you have missed the mark. Are you tired of the old life? Would you like to quit it and become a man? You know what God has done for you; you are aware that God still loves you and wants you. He has a plan and purpose yet for your life, for He so loved you that He gave His only begotten Son that you should not perish, but have eternal life. Now, Halfdan, I just want to join with you in turning to Him and asking Him to forgive you and accept you, to restore you and to come into your heart with His Spirit and make you His own, with a new will and new power.' We knelt to pray.

"God made him over that day; he was born again. I had the joy of seeing him restored, and after a period of employment sent back to his waiting mother, who had not heard from him for many years. 'Man gets and forgets; but God gives and forgives.'"

Another dream of Abram's which blossomed into a project of faith was a farm on an island, with adequate care and opportunities for agriculture, horticulture, and various crafts. The way in which it came into being was a further illustration of the balanced combination of faith and action by which the Spirit of God does the work of God through men of God. Abram's particular concern at that time were the physical, mental, and moral casualties after World War I.

"One evening," he writes, "I was invited out to dinner at the home of one of the judges of the Superior Court. He introduced me to an elderly lady, who was also a guest there that night. They wanted to hear my story about the work I was doing. In connection with that, I told them about the need for a farm. The judge informed me about such a place advertised in the paper, and that it might be well for me to look it over. I suggested that this lady could come along, so the Judge encouraged her to come, and the appointment was made for the following day. Alongside the main highway was this fifty-five acre, delightful layout, on which some $94,000 had been expended in improvement, but the investment had failed and the property had been idle for some time. There was a delightful building, orchards, fruit trees, fields, and a big canyon, with magnificent trees, springs and two streams. It was a most inviting place. After looking the premises over, I left the lady in the automobile, while I walked over among the fir trees where I could be in seclusion, and I knelt and asked God that if He wanted us to have this place for His needy children and for His glory, He would put it into the heart of this woman to put up enough money to close the deal. As I drove along with her towards the bank at Vashon, she volunteered she would give $10; but of course that was not enough. She stood nearby as I discussed the proposition with the banker, who informed me that we could have the place for $12,000, with $100 down in earnest money, $1000 within thirty days, and the balance $1000 a year. Immediately this lady spoke up and said she would put up the $100. This was God's token that the plan was His, and not mine, and that He would provide the balance. The following Wednesday I told the story to the Exchange Club, and there, without any asking from my side, they immediately volunteered to cooperate, and $1000 was raised on the spot. I telegraphed to a staunch, experienced Christian farmer in Oregon, telling him about the opportunity for service, and asking him to take hold of the management, invest his money, and give his time and talents, without any financial compensation, but that his reward would be from God. He telegraphed back that he was coming. Mr. and Mrs. Anton Larson became the greatly loved and trusted leaders of the enterprise. Youth groups and ladies' groups of the city competed in fixing up and furnishing rooms, poultry, livestock. The equipment and various supplies were obtained from different sources. Soon a great human reclamation program was under way, and the whole enterprise dedicated by the Rev. Stanley Mook."

8 | DEEPER INSIGHTS

Another great turning point in Abram's life had been reached. The first had been his emigration to America. The second was the experience gained through the Christian ministry, in the practical application of the dominating passion of his life—to bring Christ to men and men to Christ. The third, yet to come, was the channeling of this redemptive stream through him in its planned direction—chosen and called of God to it as much as Paul was to the Gentiles.

After nine years as superintendent of the Goodwill Industries in Seattle, Abram was invited to Boston in 1931 to be associate general superintendent of the Goodwill Industries of America, as well as pastor of the English Department of the Church of All Nations, and executive secretary for Goodwill Industries for New England, positions he held till 1934.

During the years of the depression, this program for stretching the dollar by turning waste into wages grew in importance. He was asked by their governors to address various conferences in the New England states—John Wilson of Vermont, Winant of New Hampshire, Ely of Massachusetts, Green of Rhode Island, Cox of Connecticut, Gardner of Maine, and to consult with men of industry. The idea was to relate the program of Good Will Industries to the employment policies of states; but in the discussions what one man said in the Senate Chamber at the State House in Montpelier of Vermont was largely representative of what he heard in each state. This man brought out that in a study of the social and economic life of the state, he had become aware of the fact that every economic depression was preceded by a period of moral and spiritual decline and neglect by the people of the church and the religious life, and that every spiritual awakening was followed by social stability, progress, and economic prosperity. The present social and economic conditions, in other words, were largely brought about through neglect of religious life. Abram had not been aware of this. He had gone to these conferences to sell Good-

will Industries, but he found himself faced with a spiritual issue. He began to see the implications of the relationship of
the political and industrial leadership of America to the social
and economic problems which they were facing. In order to
remedy the latter, it was necessary to redeem the former. It
takes kingdom of God people to do kingdom of God work.
Everybody wants the kingdom—but without the King!

The turning point came when Franklin D. Roosevelt, then
governor of New York State, invited him to a conference
concerning a social relief program for that state. (This was not
his first contact with F.D.R. On a previous visit, he had "witnessed to him about Christ as Saviour and Lord.") This conference was on Lincoln's birthday in 1932. "He wanted me to
take charge of a state program," wrote Abram, "and apply
this principle of the Good Will Industries in the expenditure of
a fund of eighteen million dollars for the state. This I didn't do,
as the religious phases could not be included; but he also emphasized that what the state needed more than anything else
was a spiritual upsurge. He called James Farrell, president of
the United States Steel Corporation, and arranged for a few
men to meet me in his office to discuss the needs of the state in
the field that was then my specialty. That meeting became a
turning point in my work.

"Mr. Farrell reviewed the history of America and pointed
out that we have had nineteen depressions—five major ones
—and that every one was caused by disobedience to divine
laws, neglect of God, the church and the spiritual life, and that
what had given rise to economic prosperity and social welfare
was the quickening of the religious life. 'Now,' said he, 'I am a
Roman Catholic and we don't go in much for revivals and
such things, but I am as sure as I am sitting here that if we
don't get a thorough revival of genuine religion, with confession of our sins and repentance toward God by high and low,
and a return to prayer and the Bible, we are headed for
chaos. It must come through laymen, and the leaders of industry and business must begin to lead.' "

A further and deeply interesting insight came to him when
Carl Vrooman of Bloomington, Ill., assistant secretary of the
Department of Agriculture under President Wilson, gave him
a special appointment after Franklin Roosevelt was nominated

for president in those dark days of the depression. F.D.R. had asked Vrooman to form an advisory group for his administration in the national policy and program. Vrooman who had just spoken for Abram at a meeting for the clergy in Boston and had found that he shared with Abram a mutual concern to save America from the political and economic breakdown that then existed, asked Abram to head the Social Service portfolio. Thus Abram was introduced to the inner workings of the economic and political forces of the nation and saw how serious was the danger of leftwing elements actually taking over the nation. This super-cabinet did not become active as the New Deal took over.

Right in the middle of these deepening concerns, God was already giving the answer through Abram's ministry—the only answer there is—and the combination of the following two incidents taking place in the same city was a wonderful silent reminder of the fact that in the light of eternity no earthly position is significant; there is neither privileged nor under-privileged, there are neither high nor low, all have sinned, all are under judgment, all must accept as little children the same saving grace of God in Christ.

Abram was visiting Detroit for the Goodwill Industries and social workers conference for the state of Michigan. Back in Seattle a meeting was held each morning at the Mission Chapel of the Goodwill Industries. One day some years before, a bushy-haired fellow dropped in and, at the end, walked up to Abram and exclaimed, "What is this now? You talked about something I know nothing about; and then you closed your eyes and began to talk as if somebody else was present. But I didn't see anybody. What sort of joint is this?" "It's the kind of place where fellows like you can find yourselves and make a success of life," responded Abram. "You say you couldn't see anybody, but that Person is real and He's here." "Where is he?" the man asked. "Well, can you see my thoughts or emotions? God is like that. He is mind and will and emotion. He made all things," announced Abram.

He found out subsequently that this man had been born in England, had never had a home, was kicked from pillar to post, spent much of his time in jail. He jumped a ship to America and became part of a gang which lived by robbery and crime. He was in Seattle for the kickoff of a bank robbery to take place two days later. He had just come in to get something to get by with till the event took place.

"Would you like to meet Him?" Abram asked then. "Sure I would." "Well, you can." And Abram told him the Gospel story. "As you kneel down with me and ask Him, you'll see what will happen. Kneel, and we will talk to Him. I first, you follow." He did so, and as they began to talk to God, the man burst out with his curse words, the only words he knew; "By God, I believe you're here." Then, "D--- it, if you can help me, please do so." Then up he jumped to his feet and shouted, "He is here! and, He is real!" After subsequent instruction, taking him to a home for homeless men and getting him a job, Abram didn't see him for several years.

But when Abram was speaking to the social workers at the Detroit conference, he used this man's story as an illustration. As soon as the meeting was over, a man in Salvation Army uniform rushed up excitedly saying, "Don't you know me?" Abram did not until he exclaimed, "I'm Jack!" Abram "hollered" out, "Here's the man I've been talking about," and as the people crowded around, Jack confirmed it. Abram knew he had been talking to many who might not have seen for themselves that Christ is the answer, and here was the exceptional chance to demonstrate it. It was, as he said to them, "A liability made asset; waste turned into wages."

At this same social workers' conference, when Abram was addressing a women's group, unknown to him Mrs. Henry Ford, the wife of Henry Ford I, was present. She was so impressed that she told her husband, who phoned and asked Abram to come and have dinner with him. After several further meetings at his office, he asked Abram to come and spend time with him alone in Sudbury, Mass., the village which he had rebuilt. They were together two days, he unloading about spiritual, intellectual and business problems, and Abram seeking to give the answer for himself and the nation. Henry Ford was so "befuddled" with all kinds of notions he had gleaned from Hindu mysticism and theosophy and various religious and philosophical concepts that the question was, How could he be untangled? At subsequent meetings in Dearborn, Abram gave him various scriptures, taking him as far as he could. One day, after prayer and preparation, Abram left him with "the ultimate of God's revelation of Himself and what He said." When Abram came to his office next time. Henry Ford gleefully called out, "Vereide, I've got it! I've got it! I found the release that you spoke of. I've made my surrender. The only thing that matters is God's will. I'm anchored in Jesus Christ."

A word that also came from God to Abram at that time and had a definite influence upon him came through Frank Buchman of the Oxford Group, as it used to be called. Both the founder and the movement have been the center of much controversy, and under their newer title of Moral Rearmament, they are in general no longer considered to be giving the Christian message, because of their elimination of Christ and the cross and the Bible from the center of their witness; but that does not alter the fact that in its earlier days, their radical challenge and uninhibited witness shook thousands of nominal Christians out of a nominal faith and into a vital experience of Christ, thousands of whom today are no longer linked with the movement, but are God's witnesses all over the world. So it was with this brief contact of Abram with Frank Buchman. When on a lecture tour to Ottawa, they were both staying at the same hotel. Recognizing the vitality of the movement Abram suggested that Buchman might be a chaplain to the Good Will Industries and bring the life-changing witness among them. "Well," said Buchman, "let's have a quiet time." Abram was not then accustomed to listening to God in that way, and when Buchman asked him, "What did God say to you?" Abram replied, "He didn't say anything." Then Frank Buchman said, "God told me, Christianize what you have. You have something to share." It was a shaft that pierced and brought Abram right back to the fundamentals of his calling, where he said superficiality and unconfessed sin had crept in. It was a renewal of cleansing and dedication, and also to a new realization of the Quiet Time as the means of listening to God and getting His guidance on all one's affairs.

9 | THE DAM BURSTS

God's life plan for Abram was now taking shape. "My call to a specific spiritual ministry was now becoming clear," he said, with the emphasis on "specific" and "spiritual." Forty-six years of preparation had gone into it. He could now begin to say as Christ said, "For this end was I born, for this cause came I into the world"—a specialist for a specialized ministry.

Concern for the "down and out" is fairly common. Their need is obvious. Concern for the "up and out" is more rare. It takes a more discerning eye to see their need, and a rare combination of compassion, boldness and right approach to meet it. True leadership demands true men. True men are God's men. God's men have come to the cross of Christ, having discovered themselves to be untrue men, and have begun a new life of which the motivating center is God in them, and not themselves. This was Abram's apostleship. A leadership led by God. Men must first have God's salvation for their own needs, and then be God's representatives to walk in His ways and act by His spirit. The greater the sphere of influence in government or industry, the more responsible they are to make it plain by their personal living, by their conduct of affairs, and by their verbal witness, that Jesus Christ as Saviour and Lord is the only answer to the human problem, and that He must be given in our era and in our tangled affairs all the lordship we His servants can give Him, while we wait for the final consummation of "a new heaven and a new earth wherein dwelleth righteousness" at His coming. As Charles Malik, the Lebanese ambassador to the U.S.A. and former president of the United Nations, recently said to Abram, "The essence of what is wanted is the overflowing life of Jesus Christ."

When he left Boston, Abram received the following letter from James M. Curley, the mayor. "August 22, 1932. Dear Sir: It is an exceedingly great pleasure as Mayor of Boston to convey to you the appreciation of the entire people for the splendid work rendered by you in behalf of the needy of our city. . . . I trust you will accept the certificate issued by the city, in recognition of your most generous contribution of time, energy, and money in a most worthy cause ... "

One further conviction of vital importance came to maturity in Vereide when he was asked for a few months by the Council of Churches in San Francisco to be in charge of their program of evangelism. He began meeting with a group of executives in the Pacific Union Club under the leadership of Judge Carruthers. These meetings brought home to him, with a certainty that was to effect his whole future ministry, that the normal church channels were not the way to reach the people he aimed to reach. Something separate from them was necessary. It would minister to all the churches, but it must be disentangled from church organization. It was necessary to reach the unchurched and expose them to the Bible and the reality of God through men of affairs in the language they could understand and in a setting where they could be uninhibited. These Union Club meetings, in fact, were a seed germ of what was to happen in Seattle and later in the Breakfast Groups.

In 1934, after these months in San Francisco, Abram returned to his own home state of Washington. But in addition to the conviction that a new approach was a necessity, he found himself confronted with a situation which overwhelmed him. He had been deeply disturbed by conditions he found in the eastern states on a leadership level, but this was greatly intensified by what he found on the Pacific Coast. It was the utter helplessness of the rank and file under the political control of subversive forces in the saddle.

"As I traveled around lecturing and as an evangelist," he said, "I saw everywhere sights that made my heart sick. Things were clearly at a low ebb. Even then, eight years before World War II, I could see that the manpower of the churches had dwindled badly, and politics seemed under the control of those who were not fit to take leadership. As I spoke at various meetings, I found selfishness literally enthroned in high places. I saw it straight through the industrial picture; I saw it in so-called Christian homes, in professional life, in the government. Those who had bothered to look below the surface knew that the leader of the most powerful political element in that sec-

tion drew his salary and took his orders from forces that were
subversive. His organization stretched out over several coun-
ties. In order to carry on, other elements had come to depend
upon deals involving rake-offs and other un-American practices. The city I was most concerned with had lost its credit.
In fact, things had gone so far in its industrial life that many
outside business interests hesitated to ship into this area
for fear of having merchandise damaged or stolen. 'B,' the
leader, had a lot of folks up in arms against him, but most of
them had now involved themselves in one way or another and
didn't dare squeal. Some played the game and liked it, and
others paid through the nose; but whether you were a business man, a contractor, or a labor leader, you went along. B's
long right arm reached out so far that he regulated property
assessments for tax purposes—you paid, or *else*! Of course a
man has to live right *in* such a situation to feel the full impact
of it. It got me down. I yearned to do something, but what?
What could one man accomplish against such odds?" The need
of a spiritual awakening and the desperate urgency of the
hour were like birth pangs in his soul. It was to him a matter of
"get revival or be damned."

Prayer was the first necessity. He thought of what George
Muller once said: "Man's extremity is God's opportunity."
"There was nothing to do except pray; but I could do that—
and I did," he said. "Crushed and burdened by this spiritual
apathy and the downgrade pace at which things were moving, I sought God, not for myself, but for my city, state and
nation. Then one day when I had been alone with Him, at
1:30 in the morning light came and a voice spoke. I began
writing down a plan of procedure which under God had been
taking form in my mind. Then I went to bed." God's day of
destiny for Vereide had come.

"The next day I went downtown," he continued, "and walking along Fourth Avenue in front of the Douglass Building in
Seattle, Major Walter Douglass, an old acquaintance, greeted
me and remarked, 'Hey, Vereide, glad to see you! Where is this
country going to anyway?' I said, 'You ought to know.' Then
he said, 'It seems to me that we are going to the bow-wows,
all of us, and the worst of it is you fellows aren't doing anything about it!'

"I said, 'What do you mean, We're not doing anything about it?' 'Well,' he said, 'here you have your churches and services and a merry-go-round of activities, but as far as any actual impact and strategy for turning the tide is concerned, you're not making a dent.' 'Well,' I said, 'what do you think we ought to do?' 'For one thing, you ought to get after fellows like me.' Then I told him what had come to me the night before, without telling him how or the background of it. (If I had, he would likely have thought that I was a bit cracked.)

"After I had spoken, he looked at me with a piercing gaze and remarked, 'Vereide, if you will settle down in this city and do a job like that, I will back you.' 'What do you mean by backing me?' said I. 'Pick out a suite of offices in the building across the street,' (he was the controlling factor of the Metropolitan Building Company), 'then come in to get a check to grubstake you.' 'Well,' I said, 'that's tangible, but let's talk it over with some others.' We talked on a moment, and then he suggested that we go and see William St. Clair, the president of the Frederick Nelson, the largest department store of the Pacific Northwest. We went right over.

"Mr. St. Clair sent others away and asked us to come in. We told him the story. And he, too, looked searchingly at me as he remarked, 'That's constructive. I'll support you.'

"He made a list of nineteen executives of the city then and there, and settled on a Thursday morning at 7:45 to invite those men for breakfast. They came. That was April, 1935.

"Only one of that party had any active church relationship, and he remarked, after my introductory message, that while he was a leader in the church, 'You fellows,' said he, 'know me from the poker table and from the cocktail lounge and from the golf course, and how the grass burns when I spit (indicating his language); but you don't know that deep in my heart I believe these things that have been spoken of. My company and the city in which I have a part would be different if I had been an active practicing Christian. And right now I take my stand before you men to acknowledge Christ as my Saviour, and to pledge you that I will begin to read a chapter of the Bible every day and to put it into practice.'

"By common consent we met the following week on the same day. They are still meeting. Men who did not want to be preached at, men who were shy about being seen in church and too ignorant about spiritual things to talk about them, began to find their way to spiritual reality, to a God who hears and answers prayer, to conscious fellowship with Him as a Father, through Jesus, the Son.

"The Bible became a living book and its teachings practical in business, government and social life. They began to discover that life was so planned that things worked normally when the precepts of Jesus were followed. We discovered that, as the eye is made for light and the ear for sound, so the human personality is made for God. We discovered that sanity and normalcy are to be Christ-like.

"This was an intimate circle. We didn't dare tell anybody what was going on, or even include anyone else. It was a sharing fellowship. The Bible was our textbook. We began to apply what we found, to our personal, domestic and business life, and relate our experiences at our breakfast meeting. They became fascinatingly real and constructively helpful. Men would drive long distances and come early in the morning, regardless of weather, in order to have their part. True, some dropped out, they wouldn't face it, but others came in.

"A special weekend huddle was held in the summer of 1935 at the Canyon Creek Lodge in the Troll House by a river in the Cascade Mountains. It represented men from the breakfast group including William St. Clair, James Pollard, President of the Seattle Gas Company; Jess Kennedy, President of the Kennedy Lumber Company; Arthur E. Langlie, then of the City Council; William Devin, an attorney; A. S. Eldridge of Eldridge Securities Corporation; Vern Samuelson, President of the Ford Agency of Port Angeles; Arthur Young of the Balfour-Guthrie Company; Chester Roberts, president of the Imperial Candy Company; Clyde Rose; Commander Byrholdt of the U.S. Navy, Fred Ernst, president of Ernst Hardware Co., and others.

"By the great stone fireplace we grouped. Each man made a moral and spiritual inventory. We faced the problems of our own city and state, and those of the nation, as well as our respective businesses. The deeper and further we went, the more we readied ourselves to face God and His word. We went on our knees to pray with a deep sense of utter helplessness. Subversive forces had taken over. What could we do, and who would dare confess it and begin to lead on for better things?

"The man who arose first from his knees that day was Arthur B. Langlie who subsequently became the mayor of the city and later the governor of the state. He stated, 'Men, it can be done and I am ready to let God use me.' 'Pop' Eldridge stated, 'And I'll support you.'

"A brief discussion followed with commitments, a sense of God, and a glow of faith. Then the tall and handsome Jess Kennedy said, 'Let's join hands in this dedication to God, each other, and the task before us, and sing "Faith of our fathers."'

> Faith of our fathers, living still,
> In spite of dungeon, fire, and sword:
> Oh, how our hearts beat high with joy
> Whene'er we hear that glorious word.
> Faith of our fathers, holy faith,
> We will be true to Thee till death.

We concluded with the Lord's Prayer.

"There was born a new regime for the city of Seattle and a new epic of the political history of the city and state. 'The breakfast group is the moral anchor of the city,' said C. Jenks of the People's National Bank. 'Men meeting around that morning breakfast table don't go out to double-cross each other. In mutual confidence we build business and community life.'

"Our group was only for executives at the start. One morning a labor leader, who had been a disturbing factor in the community, was seen at the table. He came back the next week and the next and the next. We had a talk together. The following week he sat at the head table to have a part in the meeting. The men wondered what was going to happen. A serious strike had created bitter feelings and social problems. The chairman of the employers' group was present. He and this labor leader had remained unreconciled. Suddenly Jimmy got up and said, 'You fellows know me.' Nodding to one man, 'I picketed your plant,' he said; and he pointed to another man, 'I closed your factory for months.' Then pointing to another, 'I hated you,' and he pointed to still another. They all knew he told the truth.

" 'Then, I came in here a few weeks ago,' he said, 'and I saw you fellows sitting around the table and I said to myself, *That*

is them all right, the industrial royalists. Then I saw you read
the Bible and pray, and I said to myself, *What hypocrites! Here
they act pious, and then they go out skinning us poor suckers
afterwards.* But then I listened to your conversation around the
table; I discovered your sincerity, your humility, and how absolutely honest you are. I became curious and came again.
Then I began to discover how this thing cost you something,
how you were honest in your application. I began to investigate
how you were dealing with your employees, and to what extent this thing was registering in your own businesses. Then I
came to the conclusion that if that which you are now practicing could go on and become inclusive, there would be no need
of a labor union except as a social institution. You transcend
them by the spirit that is projected into the labor relationship.
Two weeks ago I couldn't stand it any longer. I went home to
my bedroom and closed the door. I got down on my knees and
asked God to forgive me for the way I had been acting and
the spirit I had been manifesting. I come to you men this morning to ask you to forgive me, for I have been a disturbing factor
and a thorn in your flesh. I believe God has forgiven me, and
I ask you to do the same. I love labor and I am going to fight
for labor, but I am going to do it in a different spirit, for I have
accepted Jesus Christ as my Saviour and Lord, and I wish to
follow Him and do right'.

"He sat down. There was a hush, a gripping silence, and
then the sturdy, rugged capitalist who had been chairman of
the employers' committee in the big strike, got up and walked
to the head of the table, and while that distinguished group
of community leaders, numbering about seventy-five at that
time, looked on, he put his left hand on the speaker's shoulder and then reached out with his right hand to clasp the
speaker by the hand, saying, 'Jimmy, on this basis we go on together.' They held each other's hand for a moment in silence,
while they and the others present battled with their own emotions.

"They have gone on together since. It was the beginning of
better things. It was that making up with God and each other,
that was the sensible way of doing things. We found that we
had been blocking the channels for the Spirit of the Almighty
to come and work through us and with us. To be humble

58

means to be honest, to be real.

"Out of that group was born new leadership of integrity, vision and the spirit of cooperation and understanding. They discovered that it was necessary to establish a base and to become properly related as a branch in the Vine in order to produce the fruit, both in the social and economic life. The product was new men, reborn by the Word and the Spirit of God. The by-product was social, economic and political transformation, through men of goodwill and honesty. The meetings were strictly informal. Men of affairs would discuss spiritual things in a matter-of-fact way and in their own terminology. Teamwork followed. These men began to visit other cities throughout the state to tell the story.

"An army chaplain was preaching in a church at Peshastin, Washington. After attending a breakfast group meeting he invited us to bring the message to his community. The time was set. He made the arrangements. Four automobiles with four or five men in each car went. Busy business executives, who were prominently known all over the state, launching out on a missionary journey over the Cascade Mountains, was front page news. One of the men was known to have squandered a great fortune in loose living, but had become a new man, winning his butler and chauffeur for Christ, and drove his $20,000 Dusenburg car on this mission. This was a new experience for all of them. The men invited to hear them were responsible leaders from all walks of life from that whole area.

"What an exciting experience for two days! Men were quickened into a new life. A new group was born in that town and later in surrounding towns and villages. The visits were repeated to other centers until the state was pretty well covered. Each man told his story of defeat and victory, prayer and how it works, Bible reading and living it, family problems settled, employee relations ironed out and teamwork established. A new era was born in state affairs.

"The men who went out on these missions developed rapidly. A robust and healthy spiritual life was the result. There was intake and outflow, impression and expression.

"Most of the ministers were encouraged and thankful. The women, too, formed their groups for prayer, Bible study and community service—doing valiantly around election time by covering various precincts in getting people registered, informed and voting.

"When the new governor, Arthur B. Langlie, was installed in 1940, three hundred men from different parts of the state came together for breakfast with him at the State Capitol. There was no newspaper publicity. The Supreme Court and some members of both houses of the State Legislature were there. The Chief Justice read the scripture. Two men offered prayers. Representatives from both parties participated. A stirring message and testimony was given by the Governor. There were a few moments of silent prayer and dedication, and then all joined in the Lord's Prayer and in singing, 'Our father's God, to Thee, Author of liberty, to Thee we sing. Long may our land be bright, with freedom's holy light, protect us with Thy might, great God, our King.'

"Similar dedications took place in other cities and communities, as a mayor or county official was elected and would be part of this vanguard for better things. There was no formal membership and no dues. A man didn't have to take part if he didn't want to. His attitude to God and other men would determine his place and part. Many would give of their resources for specific projects and for general expenses. According to Bible instruction, some began to give one-tenth of their income to religious, civic or charitable work. We had a spiritual service center, a clinic, and a place for prayer and administration. The winds of God had begun to blow. The tide was coming in.

"Continuing with daily meetings of prayer at the office gave us constant victory.

"The dean of men at the Washington State University called one day and said that probably 95% of his students didn't attend church, and some of his brightest students were a disturbing influence on the campus because of a lack of moral restraint, as well as infiltration among them of the communist ideology. He said, 'This being a state university, we are not in a position to give any religious emphasis or project ourselves in the field, and I was wondering what you would suggest might be done.'

"'If you will select one hundred of your keenest and ablest leaders on the campus of the type you have described and give me their names and addresses,' I said, 'then I will select a group of my men whom they will be honored to sit down to dinner with, such as the sports editor of the morning paper, the mayor of the city, a superior court judge, three of our outstanding business executives, a labor leader and two men from professional life. We will arrange for the finest dining hall at a near-by hotel and we will invite these fellows to be our guests, the subject being current problems and their solution, the elder seeking the counsel of the younger.'

"He thought the idea was great. Ninety-four of the boys came. The president of the student body sat at the head of the table with the seniors. The mayor presented some of the problems of the city and then proceeded to tell them some of the steps he had been taking toward their solution. 'Now what do you think?' he asked.

"The sports editor discussed the problems in his field and brought out the answers he had found and also asked for their suggestions. The men in industry, both management and labor, did the same, and so on down the line, briefly and to the point. Each time they went a little deeper and a little farther in presenting the Bible as the textbook and the blueprint, how prayer worked, how God was real and how Jesus Christ had brought the answer to their personal problems and was a living Companion in everyday affairs.

"Their messages were delivered in a matter-of-fact manner; there was nothing preachy or pious. It was simple and natural, factual and personal.

"The chairman then asked for the opinion of the students. The president of the combined student organizations was the first speaker. 'I am a Jew,' said he, 'but what I have heard tonight overwhelms me. I have read something about Nehemiah and some prophets in olden days who had some contact with the Almighty, but I didn't think anything like this would be possible today. If these statements hadn't come from men like you, whom I am honored to sit down with, whose intelligence, training and integrity I admire, I would not have believed what you have said. This must be true—this must be the answer. I guess I have missed the boat.' His emotions overwhelmed him and he sat down.

"One after another of the young fellows participated and

expressed their appreciation, and some their determination to go back and find the Bible and begin life on the same basis.

"The following week the dean of men called me, stating that these fellows would like to begin similar groups to those in operation among the older men. These groups continued with great effectiveness until World War II scattered the boys."

But this did not mean that Abram ceased to carry the burden for the movings of the Spirit in the city. In his new offices he had daily prayer periods. He started alone, and there was not a day, he said, in which he was not broken up and in tears with the burden.

One incident greatly impressed him. When particularly tried and tested, as he wept and prayed, with satanic forces seeming so entrenched and the churches seeming so indifferent, in walked a Pentecostal pastor named Henry Ness. He told Vereide that he and his people had been praying for him, and that he knew his work was of God. The point was that Vereide had disliked Ness and had condemned and opposed his work, especially as Ness had taken some of his own congretion. The fact that this man and his people had been praying for him, and that it had been revealed to them that the work was of God, simply broke Abram.

The spirit of prayer now began to increase. People began to come without announcement or invitation—first one room full, then two rooms, then three. There was no preaching, only prayer, and "such a power of the Holy Spirit rested upon us for revival in Seattle and the northwest."

All who started, of course, did not continue. Some dropped back. They couldn't pay the price and clean up. Men recognized what was needed, but they were not ready for the cost of discipleship. "It was a heart-breaking time," said Abram. They personally loved him, but could not go with him.

When C. B. Hedstrom, president of the Christian Businessmen's Committee in Chicago, heard what was happening, he paid them a visit. This resulted in the beginning of a group of Christian laymen in Seattle, inaugurated by the CBMC with Vereide as executive secretary. Daily noon meetings were begun in the leading theater, the Metropolitan, a beautiful building, with one of the Breakfast Group men giving $50 a day for the expenses. Abram was responsible for the two meetings for about a year, the breakfast group at City Chapel and the CBMC meeting at the theater, with Dr. N. A. Jepson as chairman. Revival broke out. As many as two-hundred people accepted Christ at a noon day session, filling the stage. Visiting evangelists came, eliminating everything denominational or sectarian, and just presented the claims of Jesus Christ, calling men to repentance and faith in Him.

Then one man came who attacked certain parts of the church and preached schismatic doctrine. It was as though the Holy Spirit had withdrawn. Vereide resigned, and the theater services were discontinued, but later resumed on a modified scale.

"The lesson we need to learn," commented Abram on the tragedy, "is to preach Christ and the centrality of the Gospel without sectarian doctrines or attacks on others." And in later years, commenting on the Breakfast Groups, he put it in this way: "While I am a genuine evangelical, the evangelical groups have often wanted to take the Breakfast Groups and convert them true to type and to their cliches. I want them and want their group; but sometimes they don't understand and want to hamstring the Holy Spirit. The wind bloweth where it listeth, but men want to *control what they can't produce.* How easy it is to divide the flock, and fail in understanding and patience with one another, instead of humbly recognizing our limitations. We see in part, and understand in part, even when we all want Jesus and seek to be true to the Word."

10 | COUNTING THE COST

The winds of the Spirit were plainly blowing, and God's seal was on the Breakfast Group. But as it is with every step of obedience to God there were new sacrifices to make, new strains and stresses on the normal routine of life. The law of spiritual harvest remains unchanged: "Except a corn of wheat fall into the ground and *die,* it abideth alone; but if it die, it bringeth forth much fruit." The security of a regular salary may have to be exchanged for the apparent uncertainty of "living by faith"; the togetherness of a happy home may have to be disrupted by many long absences; the final decision may have to be made, whether God's calling is the uprooting of wife and children to move out to an unknown and insecure future. From their family home to where? From a community where they are loved and honored, from a work which is established and successful, to what? Nothing much more than a vacuum . . . but with God!

As Abram said later, "Then and during subsequent years, again and again there was the pressure to leave this and go back to the security and comfort of a settled position; but the word of Jeremiah 1:7, 'Say not, I am a child, for thou shalt go to all that I shall send thee': and God's call to keep steady under pressure and faithful to the calling, although alone and misunderstood: His personal word to me, 'Attend to the business to which I have called you, regardless of circumstances': and the reminder of the word when I first arrived in the USA, 'There is yet the future, and your hope will not come to naught.': these held me.

"The battle through the years! Wife wanting home, security, retirement pension. Hold on to what you've got, instead of launching out on the unknown. It was an awfully lonely life, with very few days without tears."

Such a move is not made lightly, not without a clear sense of guidance; a servant has a right to orders, how much more the servants of the Lord Christ.

The steps with Abram were gradual, first there were "journeyings oft" with their many absences; then the moving of the office to Chicago; then the home to Chicago; and finally, office and home to Washington, D. C. These many absences from home began a series of letters to his wife, and a true man is what he really is when he writes to his wife.

Davenport Hotel, Spokane, Washington

9-13-34

I am thinking about you and picture you about in our cozy little home. Glad and thankful that God gave you to me. The one great regret is that I haven't been a better husband. Your patience and love shall be rewarded. You have your hands full with all the company Sunday. That is just like you—think of others, serve, help and gladden. I preach and you practice. Well, I try to live it too.

A month later
Davenport Hotel, Spokane, Washington.

At Centenary Church we have some few witnesses each evening, and we are building a work group in the church that will carry on personal work. Last week you received $10 only. This week will be more substantial. Then it costs me very little. I do count the pennies, that I may do my best for you. It was such a good thing that you took over the treasurership of the Co.

Davenport Hotel, Spokane, Washington

B—is nice—but oh, Mattie mine, oh, Mattie mine! You compare with the best. God bless and preserve you for many years of happy life together. Just a week and I am, God willing, home with you again. Well, I'm having victory both within and without. Praise God!

In the New Year, 1935
Bruce Hotel, Wenatchee, Washington:

New Year, 1935
"The first letter of the new year must, of course, be to you. My heart overflows in love for and appreciation of you. My first prayer as I knelt at my bed in my pajamas this morning was for a happy new year to you—and ours —and that I might help to make it so, by *being* and *doing*. Had a good service last night. Afterward I walked by a pentecostal church and went in. Earnest and well-meaning folk they were. God bless them. I do love them and all who love Christ. Then I walked about town, looked in on a hilarious group drinking and dancing, talked to a young fellow and invited him to church, then to my room to thank God for the year, His grace, love, care and keeping. Trusting in Jesus and His blood to cleanse me from *all sin* and committing you all to His care.

"I have smoked salmon aplenty—guess where I have been. Really, I had forgotten that John Anderson was here. So I went down to the market and ate smoked salmon—then he took some fresh rock cod and soles into an adjoining restaurant and had it prepared for me—and oh did I eat? He is going to send some home with me.

"I feel quite confident that the most economical deal we could make was that which we did as far as the car is concerned. So thank God and be happy. It is *His* car to *His* glory and for *His* work."
And three days later:

"How I do look forward to being home more! What a balance wheel you are and have been! May we now together proceed to build the most ideal home life possible. The dinner hour is the richest opportunity—fellowship, joy, sharing of experiences and Bible and prayer—making it mean more and more, to strengthen and help the children. Then in it all—love, cherish, cheer, gladden, protect and enjoy my own darling Mattie."

Calls for breakfast groups began to come from other cities. Judge Curtis Wilbur, former Secretary of the Navy, visited Seattle and attended one of the breakfasts. "This is what we need in San Francisco," he said. Some of them responded to his invitation, and a group was inaugurated in the Olympic Club.

Then Mayor LaGuardia of New York attended one of the meetings in San Francisco a little later and said, "This is what we need in New York. Will you help us to get going?" An oil engineer from Los Angeles, Van Moulton, attended a meeting and said, "This is what we need in Los Angeles. Come and help us." A representative from Wasington, D.C. attended and said, "This is what we need in the Congress and in every department of our national life." A group of men met for a retreat at the Lake Shore Club in Chicago, and from that was born the first Chicago breakfast group. Allan Emery of Boston invited a body of men to the Boston City Club to hear the story, and a group was started there. Dr. Dan Poling met a man on the train who told him about the transforming influence of the group in Seattle, and later, after a visit, he started a unit in Philadelphia. Dr. John Evans of Baltimore attended a meeting and began a group in that city which still continues under his devoted and capable leadership.

One personal contact that Vereide made at that time was with Dr. Paul Cadman, head of the department of economics at the University of California at Berkeley. On one of Abram's visits to San Francisco, he was calling on men in their offices and talked to them about the problems of the nation and God's plan through men who can be agents for Him and through whom He could work. One of those who had previously made his commitment to Christ was the president of Standard Oil in California. He insisted to Abram, "I don't want you to leave San Francisco without meeting Paul Cadman, the most brilliant man here, the economic advisor to a group of capitalists in the Bay area. He needs what you've got." Abram didn't want to meet an intellectual of that caliber, but this man had phoned and made the appointment before he could refuse. Cadman was one of those men who appear to scoff at the supernatural and the reality of prayer or God or the Bible. So when Vereide referred to spiritual realities, Cadman was very elusive and "superior." But when the conversation turned to the actualities of life, he acknowledged that he didn't know the solution for himself and his own domestic problems, nor for the men he was there to advise. Their problems were deeper and more far reaching than he could tackle. Abram then boldly presented Jesus Christ and His claims, and that if any man is willing, he shall know. This was a matter of factual demonstration. Jesus Christ invites us and says, "Come unto me all ye that labour. . . ." We can do what He says and find out for ourselves. Abram challenged him to do this, to recognize that Jesus Christ is the only One in history who lived what He taught. In His life was no discrepancy. He is the only universal, belonging to all ages, races, and conditions; His example and precepts meet the need everywhere. To be honest we must face Him and meet His challenge. "Dr. Cadman," he said, "will you come with me to meet Him?" Cadman paused a moment and answered, "I will." Then they prayed. "In my prayer and his," Abram said, "we had a sense of meeting with God" as Abram quoted, "Him that cometh to me I will in no wise cast out." Cadman then said, "Will you call me Paul and may I call you Abram, and will you help me in this new basis of life?" "So we found together," commented Abram, "the anchorage for faith in the Bible, and comfort and inspiration through prayer, and encouraging results through practice of what the Bible teaches and the Holy Spirit directs. Dr. Paul Cadman became the economic counsellor to the American Bankers Association with a new note, a new emphasis in his messages."

11 | AUDACIOUS FAITH

The year 1941, that year of grave events in the national life, the year of Pearl Harbor, was as the voice of God to Vereide, summoning him to take his boldest step of faith. It came strongly to him that now, if ever, "members of Congress needed to know each other on a spiritual basis and to find a comradeship based on mutual relationship to a heavenly Father. Everyone needed the guidance, wisdom and power of God."

But how to make an inroad on Washington? How to contact the leaders of the nation? Where to begin? "I was not my own," writes Abram. "I turned to God. This was His business. Jesus said, 'As my Father sent me, so have I sent you'; and said He about Himself, 'He that sent me is with me.' He had told us to go and declared, 'Lo, I am with you alway.' I could depend upon Him."

So an insignificant total stranger from the Pacific Coast made arrangements at the Willard Hotel in Washington for a breakfast one morning for one hundred men, and then proceeded to issue invitations to members of the Senate and the House of Representatives and a few others, making personal calls on some of them.

"It is with eagerness that I now face Washington with a renewed dedication to the task before me," he wrote his wife on Sept. 6, 1941. "Reading from Galatians 4 and 5 about my sonship, I know that my heavenly Father will take care of me and direct my steps. To Him I commit you—and all of you—constantly."

University Club, Washington

Sept. 6, 1941

Well here I am finally at the terminal of my journey.
It is an old building, staid, comfortable but not up to date.
The weather is fine and the city is attractive—now some
over 1 million people. Only God can make a dent upon
the worldly-minded, defense-occupied leadership. But,
blessed be His name, all things are possible with God!
In a day or two—many will know that I am in town and
by God's grace it will hum.

University Club, Washington

Sept. 9, 1941

95° and up in the shade—muggy heat, sweating much,
but I am well and happy in the Lord. My first appointment is here for breakfast with Col. Brindley and then
8 o'clock with congressmen. Spent all forenoon yesterday with congressmen and senators. We will have a good
delegation from there, then out to other offices—till I was
all soaked with perspiration and came in to cool off and
clean up—as well as recharge my own batteries. They
have been very cooperative. What a privilege to get ac-
quainted and have this chance! Next door to the club is
the stately Russian Embassy. Across the street is the
beautiful headquarters of the National Geographic Society.
National and international life is centered here and people
are flocking in here from everywhere. So many interesting
people and situations. The mother to the president passing
away will delay my visit with him. But that's all in the
Lord's hands. How blessed to *commit all* to Him.

He asked Francis Sayre, who had recently returned as high
commissioner to the Philippines, and Howard B. Coonley,
president of the National Association of Manufacturers, who
was in the city at the time, to join him, the one to preside
and the other to bring a message.

The breakfast was in the New Year. "It was a wintry morning
in January, 1942, and a heavy snowfall tied up the traffic. I
had to walk from the University Club, where I was staying as
the guest of Colonel Brindley, to the hotel. Seventy-four men

came. Both Mr. Coonley and Mr. Sayre gave splendid messages. I told the story of the Breakfast Groups and suggested to members of the Congress that they begin to meet in a similar fashion and set the pace for our national life, in order that we might be a God-directed and God-controlled nation, recalling what William Penn said: 'Men must either be governed by God or ruled by tyrants.' "

The next week a group was inaugurated in the Speaker's dining room of the House of Representatives. Later a similar group was begun in the Vandenburg Room of the Senate restaurant, for senators only. Colonel Brindley started a group at the University Club, and later a group began to meet at the Statler Hotel—"an informal association of responsible laymen banded together for mutual study and comradeship, to find through Christ the better way of everyday living, and to promote for home, community and nation a more effective Christian leadership."

In his letters to Mattie, Abram was constantly sharing his experiences of the next two years, before the final decision to move was taken. It was living in a suitcase, crossing and recrossing the country:

The Olympian, The Milwaukee Railroad. Enroute
                                              April 17, 1942
We will be in Montana till about 9 in the morning. I always enjoy coming into Montana—where I found you. Then I live over the old memories. They are good and happy memories. You are at the center of them.

Now at Deer Lodge, Mont. We have been up in the snow—now over bleak and barren region where we do not see any evidence of spring yet. But we are approaching dear old Butte—Do you remember?

I can sense upon me the presence and blessing of God—as the people are praying for me.

Union League Club of Chicago, Chicago, Ill.
                                              November 9,1942
I have been around as usual making several calls and having a success. God is working through me. I listen to His voice and go as He directs me. There are times when

I make a mistake and follow my own inclinations, but most of the time it is God. For I am His man. I am here to *do His will.*

Union League Club of Chicago, Chicago, Ill.
November 11, 1942

Chester Creider of the Br. Group came here at 7:30 and now it is 10 a.m. It has been a fruitful morning. He made a full surrender. Praise God! The days are full and rich. The men here are more hospitable and helpful than any places I have been.

Union League Club of Chicago, Chicago, Ill.
November 15, 1942

The trip to Washington was successful and I am thankful for it. On the way home I had the joy of pointing a man to Christ. He is born and raised in Wash., D.C. and works for the Reconstruction Finance Corporation of the U.S.A., on his way to Seattle for a few days.

Hotel Californian, San Francisco, Cal.
December 13, 1942

In my selfishness I crave to have you more constantly with me—to be alone with you and enjoy nature, books, music, song and life as a whole; but then I remember life is service and sacrifice.

Hotel Washington, Washington, D.C.
Jan. 11, 1943

This is the most crucial year in our history as a nation. Whatever sacrifices we can make and whatever we can do—we should do. I feel so humble and little and unworthy—but here I am in the providence of God. The big men and real leaders in New York and Chicago look up to me in an embarrassing way. In the morning I meet first with Senate and then the House.

The Columbian, B. O. Railroad, Enroute
Jan. 19, 1943

This parlor car is filled with all kinds of men—but all men. What faces to study! I would like to know them. May God use me to introduce men to Christ!

University Club, Washington

Jan. 22, 1943

It is a cold and pleasant morning, my first at the U. Club. I spent the whole day on the hill—that's the Capitol. Just now Vice President Wallace came in to play squash—I had a few words with him. He invited me to ride to the Capitol with him. That's God's leading. Last night I was so dead tired that I wasn't able to write to you. I had been talking all day—going from man to man. God is leading and opening the way.

7 p.m. My what a full and busy day! The Vice President brought me to the Capitol and counseled with me regarding the program and plans, and then introduced me to Senator Brewster, who in turn to Senator Burton—then planned further the program and enlisted their cooperation. Then to the Supreme Court for visits with some of them and secured their presence and participation—then back to Senate, House—and lunch with Chaplain Montgomery. Now to dine with Col. Brindley and Col. Hill, then Mr. Brason is coming with him to a meeting, then a committee in a home, etc. My appointments begin at 8:30 tomorrow and then all day. The breakfast is Thursday at Willard Hotel Congressional room. The hand of the Lord is upon me. He is leading.

Saturday evening—8. All is well. But I get so little sleep and I get very tired. Praise God for His leading and care. He certainly has guided my steps. The prospects are for a very fine meeting Thursday. How many interesting interviews—and some very hard ones. The need here is very great. I really ought to remain for a while to get the work firmly going. It is hard to remain without closer contact with home. Mattie, dear, you and the children and grandchildren are so exceedingly precious to me. I like the city and God has many of his own even here where so much wickedness goes on.

University Club, Washington

Jan. 28, 1943

Deep snow, ice and blockages. But even so we had a fine —very good—B.G. this morning. The program was given a good send off by Col. Hill of the General Staff of the Army, High Com. Sayre—who gave a great message. Several senators and congressmen spoke.

I had an appoinment with the Crown Prince for 11 a.m. today at the Norwegian Legation—The Embassy. I was with him for 35 minutes. It was a good visit. We had prayer.

University Club, Washington

Jan. 31, 1943

The Club is a pleasant place to stay—men only. I know several men here now, so it is good that way. God used me to lead a student from M.I.T. of Boston to Christ Friday. He expects to arrange for a student meeting there Monday the 8th.

United States Senate, Washington

Feb. 3, 1943

It has been two eventful weeks here packed with work.This program is now before the nation in a new way. I will write the whole Congress personal letters from Chicago. Preparation work is now under way in each city that I go to. I have to carry with me the old correspondence and plans and at the same time the preparations and program ahead. If I only had a secretary!

Hotel New Yorker, New York

Feb. 5, 1943

How I wish you were with me now! Yet this confinement may be just what I need—alone with God and recharge the batteries. For I was run down. There was little sleep at Washington and a constant drain. So much to accomplish in so short a time.

National Committee for Christian Leadership, Chicago

April 29, 1943

We had a most outstanding Breakfast this morning. A blessed and powerful meeting. I was in prayer till early morning. "These things," said Jesus, "are not accomplished except by prayer and discipline." A new group will begin at Oak Park next week. Thank God, it is moving. One man was converted in my room last night. Spiritual results is the big thing.

En route New York

May 13, 1943

It is a beautiful day. My heart is filled with joy and praise. The trip and task at Washington is done. It has been very successful. This morning's meeting has been the best ever. What a spirit and victory! The senators were so happy and grateful too. Former president and present president of U.S. Chamber of Commerce are members of the group, President American Federation of Labor, etc.

Had a good meal on the train and dealt with a man across the table. Trust God will bless the seed sown. Two Negro maids were cleaning out the room as I came in— had prayer with them. They said that I was the first white man Christian they had met. Here is much stir and interest over Tunisia victories and Churchill conference and many other things—would to God they would begin to stir for Christ and the salvation of souls.

Just read over your letter again—and again. We are *bound* together—in home—children, mutual interests, hopes and spirit. Thank God for you, dear. Last night I read and prayed in bed or on my knees till 2:30 a.m. It was such a burden for the work and especially the meeting this morning. When God gave me victory, peace and joy flooded my soul and I slept till 6:30 a.m. Then to the Senate. I was so at ease and assured of victory.

Book-Cadillac Hotel, Detroit, Michigan

May 19, 1943

Luncheon with President Coyle of the Chevrolet Automobile Co. and Harvey Freelauff, President of the Freelauff Trailer Co. from 12 till 3:15.

Business men are greatly concerned about the future. How great to know God and His plans! Again and again I find myself saying, "Praise God I am saved, in His keeping and in the embrace of His love. Mr. Ford is ill, so is his son Edsel. May God bless them with His peace and saving grace."

Hotel New Yorker, New York

June 25, 1943

Mr. Watson, president of International Business Machinery Corp. and president of the International Chamber of Commerce, has called a few of New York's top men for a luncheon Monday at the Bankers Club to meet and hear me. It seems so impossible that such should be me. I was lonely and a little downcast this morning for the task in prayer and God told me to call this man. I did and got an appointment with him at 3:30 which lasted till 5—this resulted in the luncheon for Monday.

New York is an awful mad rush with crowds, crowds everywhere, joy and sorrow, love and hate, touches of home and harmony here and there, but evidence of much sin and tragedy. Thank God for His presence here too —yes here in my room. We talk together. "He that sent me is with me."

Union League Club of Chicago

July 4,

I was thinking today of the importance of Bible reading and meditation. Please encourage our dear Jr. to regularity in this matter. He must become a boy of *the Book*. "Thy word have I hid in my heart that I should not sin against thee."

Union League Club of Chicago

July 9, 1943

Finances. The all important thing is to produce spiritual fire brands and vital groups; but a central missionary fund is needed. This work will be demanding increasing correspondence and printed material. I will have to provide that. But I know that the Lord will lead and show me His plan—step by step. When I get tired or self-centered, I want to leave it all and go home. But when I pray and get *His* touch, the burden and the vision is upon me.

Union League Club of Chicago

July 11, 1943

Mattie, can't you get a Kodak picture or some photograph of yourself? I want to show my wife—and look at her too. In fact I ought to have the whole family. Last night I prayed till 1 a.m. Some mornings I am up real early to pray. Victory is through prayer and faith.

Union League Club of Chicago

July 14, 1943

Prepared for the big event Monday Luncheon. I must be at my best physically, mentally and spiritually.

If you had been at the meeting yesterday noon—you would have been greatly stirred and pleased. First the testimonies and messages, then the testimonies of your husband. Congressman Busbey reporting how respected, loved and admired your husband was there and the contribution he had made to Congress. Also similar testimonies from men in Chicago.

Hotel New Yorker

July, 1943

My socks needed mending badly both in the heel and the toe, so I proceeded to do that in my upper berth.

Hotel Finlen, Butte, Montana

July 27, 1943

It was in this town where I first laid my eyes on you. What a day! You have held me ever since.

The Empire Builder, Great Northern Railway, enroute
December 29, 1943

Read the letter of Jude, rested, prayed, dressed and at breakfast pointed a man from Alaska to Christ. Montana looks good to me. This is the section where we were in the romantic days of 1910. As we come to the proximity of Kalispell, I will be living over again the events of long ago. Praise God, you are still with me, and by His grace we will enjoy each other and fellowship together yet for years to come—and throughout the ages. What a comfort to have Junior home—and such a fine son. It is good that we have Alicia and her children near by. Thank God for them all.

12 | GOD-GUIDED CONTACTS

It had now become obvious, with all these developments, that Seattle was too far west to be an effective base. A group of men had already incorporated the Breakfast Groups under the title of The National Committee for Christian Leadership (N.C.C.L.), for the promotion and co-ordination of the work, and the publishing of necessary material. Vereide was asked to be Executive Director, resigning from the City Chapel in Seattle, and moving to Chicago.

In 1943 he removed the office to Chicago, and in 1944 his wife and family joined him. The provision of a house in wartime was a miracle. They drove from the West, but with no certain prospect of a home. All that Abram had done was to write to his friend Harold Benson in Chicago. They reached western Illinois, stayed the night with friends, and found that Benson had sent a note to this town saying that there would be a flat available the next day. It just fitted exactly. As Vereide said, "step by step . . . the steps of faith."

But Chicago was only a break in the journey. God had life-lines prepared which were leading to the heart of the nation's capital. Abram's cross-country trips took him frequently to New York, and there he renewed contacts with a kindred spirit, Sam Shoemaker of Calvary Episcopal Church, Gramercy Park. Though Sam is an Episcopalian Rector, no one could be more outgoing, ecumenical and undenominational in his outreach. Hundreds of lives were being changed through his Calvary House conferences. He had already met Abram and seen the potential of this new move of the Spirit and had shown his interest. Abram became a frequent visitor at what he called "that world-training center, Calvary House," finding Sam "a source of help and inspiration, kindling the fire of a vital faith through his own personal experience of God's power."

From Calvary House, New York, the line of God's guidance ran straight down to the most strategic location in America for Christian witness—to Massachusetts Avenue in Washington, often called Embassy Row, where almost every nation in the world has its imposing, and sometimes ornate, embassy.

Marian Johnson of New York and Newport, Rhode Island, had the same vision and calling as Abram, though from a very different background. After her father's death, she and her mother, Mrs. Charles Frederick Hoffman, had lived at Blickling Hall, a Tudor mansion in Norfolk, England, which was the reputed birthplace of Ann Boleyn, where fox hunting and politics were her special interest. She returned to the U.S.A. to marry Aymar Johnson of the New York Stock Exchange, settling with him at Woodland, Islip, Long Island, and cruising abroad a good deal in their yacht, *The Enchantress*. She was a second cousin of Franklin Roosevelt, and she and her husband used to visit him on occasions at the White House. But life had no real meaning for her, until she met Sam Shoemaker and the group at Calvary House. "I attended the services and the meetings," she says, "and later through my surrender to Christ found the answer to my own needs—to the problems of fear, insecurity, difficult relationships and the need for forgiveness. I gave Him my all and discovered and *knew* that Jesus was a living Person and Lord. It was then that I touched reality and found there was Someone who cared and who had a plan and purpose. It was the greatest experience of my life." After that, the purpose was never in doubt—to share with others what she had found for herself and draw them too into fellowship with Him. The plan unfolded.

During World War II, Aymar Johnson needed to be in Washington, as he worked back and forth for his old friend, F.D.R., helping Admiral Jules James to establish the U.S. Naval Base in Bermuda. They could not get a house in war-time Washington, so were living in General Marshall's home, Dodona Manor, at Leesburg, Virginia. But on a visit to town, Marian came to stay with a friend from England, Col. Sir Vivian Gabriel, on Sheridan Circle and Massachusetts Avenue, the very corner on which the Fellowship House of International Christian Leadership now stands. Then and in Leesburg she had a vision from God of a fellowship house where one could have international Christian meetings—little thinking that she was looking out on the very house God had planned for this!

Her husband died in 1942, and she asked God where He wanted her to go. She checked her guidance with Sam Shoemaker and Dr. Glenn Clark, "old and new friends," and they concurred with her feeling that she was called to live in Washington, take a house, and make her home a center for personal Christian work and international fellowship meetings.

In 1943 she moved with her aunt, Miss Alice Preston of London, her daughter Moira, and her secretary, Miss Ann Gill, into 2523 Massachusetts Avenue. This was God's living link. Her home, with its spacious drawing room, became the center she hoped it would be, where many found fellowship and light. Each New Year, "The Twelve" held a retreat there, leaders of various Christian movements. They included Dr. E. Stanley Jones, Dr. Shoemaker, Dr. Rufus Jones, Dr. Frank Laubach, Dr. Glenn Clark, Starr Daily, the Rev. John Magee (the Rector of the President's church), Congressman Walter Judd, the Rev. Sherry Day and others.

Marian Johnson first heard of Vereide at Calvary House, when having dinner with Helen Shoemaker and her father, Senator Alexander Smith. Sam came in from the conference meeting downstairs and said, "You *should* have heard that fellow Vereide." Helen perked up and said, "Why didn't you warn us? I was there and left." To which Sam replied, "My dear, you always keep the best dish for the last."

Marian was not unprepared, therefore, when there was a ring at her doorbell in Washington, in January 1944, and the visitor announced, "I am Abram Vereide. Sam Shoemaker asked me to call on you." "I looked him up and down in his light blue suit," she comments. "The impression I got was of strength, simplicity and childlike faith, Norwegian blue eyes, ruddy color, and even more rugged in those days." She invited him to stay to dinner with Captain (now Rear-Admiral) Campbell-Walter of the Royal Navy and his wife, who were staying with her, and the latter commented to her afterwards— in complete bewilderment, "I think he's the most extraordinary man I ever met!"

The contact meant much for the future. Through the years of the birth and growth of International Christian Leadership

(I.C.L.) which was the final name given to the original N.C.C.L., and the maturing of Abram Vereide as God's ambassador to the leaders of nations, he and Mattie Vereide have had no more devoted friend and co-worker than Marian Johnson. The winds of God surely blow where they list, linking together in this specialized ministry one from the sheepfolds of Norway with his wife and daughter, and one nurtured in the affluence and culture of American and English society. God is no respector of persons for the simple reason that persons only exist to be reflectors of *the* Person, each in the mold of his human personality and culture pattern. On that basis, numerous natural opposites are the varied colored threads of the one divine tapestry.

Indeed it would not be a complete record of the dealings of God with Abram unless the help that Marian Johnson was to him in teamwork in those early days was mentioned. She had seen the Lord in him—a spiritual spearhead. He took over from her the idea of a vital center in Washington for international fellowship and dispensing hospitality for God to government leaders. It was also good for him to develop teamwork with others as he had had to shove on alone for so many years, although it was not easy for him to form a team and hold himself to it.

In the unity of their vision, Marian Johnson opened her home to I.C.L. activities. The meetings were led by young Professor Sverre Norborg, former professor of philosophy in the University of Minnesota and later head of U.N.R.A. in northern Europe, and Dr. Philip Marshall Brown, former professor of International Law at Princeton; Vereide would give a message. In wartime Washington, the audience was varied and included many in the Services. A contributing factor to these occasions was Miss Rosalie Leslie, assistant dean of women at Maryland University, who brought her young students, and from these Abram formed a witness team that took part in the annual I.C.L. meetings.

In December, 1944, the Vereide family moved from Chicago to Chevy Chase, a suburb of Washington, and took office quarters at 744 Jackson Place in Washington. That was even more of a miracle in war days where not a house was to be found in the capital. But God supplied through Dr. Norborg.

He told Abram that they were moving from Chevy Chase and their house would be available. He would have heat on and everything ready. As he moved out on Christmas Eve, 1944, the Vereide family arrived, having crossed the mountains in a snowstorm.

As we have already said, such moves, whether from Seattle to Chicago, or Chicago to Washington, were not lightly made. They were the obedience of faith, as much as the Abraham of the Bible, who "went out, not knowing whither he went." It meant leaving in middle age the securities of assured salary, pension and home, stepping out on nothing certain beyond the promises of God; but it is just such actions which have characterized God's special men through history, giving them the detachment and daring to be and do the unusual. It is Christ's standard of discipleship in Luke 14:33: "Whosoever he be of you that forsaketh not all that he hath, he cannot be my disciple."

The living sources of his own faith are recorded in his journal for December 31 of that same year: "Thank God for 1944 and all He has taught me. I praise Him for adoption into His family, regeneration by the Holy Spirit, the new birth through faith in and acceptance of the Lord Jesus Christ as my Saviour from sin and the Lord of my life in all areas, for cleansing through His blood and for the indwelling fullness of the blessed Holy Spirit. He guides me, comforts and strengthens me. It is grace, grace, infinite grace. As far as I know, I am utterly committed to Him. I ask for nothing but grace to do His will and glorify His name, who had redeemed me by His precious blood. With all my heart I praise Him! Amen." He adds from Goethe what appears to have been the motto for the year. "Epochs of faith are epochs of fruitfulness. Epochs of unbelief, however glittering, are barren of all permanent good."

13 | LETTERS REVEAL THE MAN

Abram's letters to Mattie throughout this critical year of 1944 reveal what the staccato entries in his journal never do.

The living Abram is talking. The letters flow like a river, through changing scenes and changing conditions—the rush of the rapids, the roar of the cataract, the onward movement through canyons of difficulty or pastures of success. Like a moving picture that jumps from subject to subject and place to place—Abram to Mattie, and sometimes Mattie to Abram: the conflicts, the doubts, the temptations to turn back: home and health problems, financial upsets, tears, prayers and praises: the set purpose of a servant of Jesus Christ, the assurances that the Lord is with him: and overflowing all, the overwhelming objective of it all, Christ for all men, from senator to bell boy. The letters must be read in one stream—as they were written:

"The Breakfast Groups" of Chicago

1-5-44

I have lunch with Sigurd Blum. Have had two prayer sessions here today, and seek to deal with someone each day. May God use me to win Sigurd—my old Sunday School boy.

Union League Club of Chicago

1-6-44

Lunch with Sigurd. He accepted Christ.

Union League of Chicago

6-1-44

From 9:30 till 10:30 I was with John Stewart, president Quaker Oats Company. I believe God has given me that man for Himself and also to this program. Mr. Cunningham, my vice president, wants me to go to Milwaukee to meet the president of the largest manufacturing company there and get a Breakfast Group going.

Edgewater Beach Hotel, Chicago

1-7-44

This has been a very good day and a fine dinner meeting to-night. They make too much of me. I don't like it. This is probably the most delightful place I ever stayed in.

The meetings have been deeply spiritual and encouraging. $12,500.00 subscribed to national program. Praise God.

Edgewater Beach Hotel, Chicago

1-9-44

I expect to go to Washington, D.C. where an important and difficult job waits me. Please pray much for me.

From *Mattie* to Abram:

1-11-44

We are proud of you—your children have something to look up to—to live up to. Well it's all by God's grace—and a gifted personality. I wish your wife had some of it but she does have some common sense, I think, and that's all.

From Abram:

Hotel Washington, Washington, D.C.

1-13-44

Last night I had dinner at a real British home, 2523 Massachusetts Avenue, N.W. A large beautiful home of three full floors with elevator. She is a widow living there with her daughter, aunt, and a British Captain and his wife. I enjoyed it much. We will have a retreat conference there January 19th for members of House and Senate. We will also hold our International Round Table there twice a month. Dr. Norborg and this Mrs. Johnson will have charge of details. This afternoon I have been in conferences with members of the House of Representatives. Praise God that I am so welcome. I know this move was right and will work out for the glory of God and our good. Be cheerful and confident of this. I hope you will come with me soon. Personal correspondence, telephone appointments, mailing and general secretarial work you could do. And Oh —to be with you! Just now what fellowship! Meanwhile you get things in order there and I will do the same here. An apartment is waiting for us in Chicago.

From *Mattie* to Abram

1-15-44

Your dream has been realized—I realize but it sure upsets me. I should be very proud of you for what you have accomplished—of course; but we felt so snug with a home and a good job on which we could begin to take things easy—at our age—and here you tackle even bigger things. I know you would rather die in the harness—fighting for God—so I should just leave it there—and God will take care of it all. I have not told anyone—I did not feel able to discuss it—I felt so shaky about it. I trembled all day—I wish you would not release it until you get home—as I don't think I can take it alone.

With a heart that is true I'll be waiting for you, Yours, Mattie.

From Abram:
Hotel Washington, Washington, D. C.

1-16-44

Had a call from Lord Halifax asking me to the British Embassy at 10:30 in the morning. Praise God for the way *He* is opening doors.

Hotel Washington, Washington, D.C.

1-16-44

This has been a heavy day and I am very tired. First, the meeting in the State Department and to the House, interviews, telephoning and a group for lunch. All afternoon till 5:30 House and Senate. Thank God for the responses. He does use me.

I am glad Doug is staying on. I will rejoice in his success and the continuous progress of the work. It is the Lord's work. We are His instruments. I have been proud and possessive about City Chapel. It was mine rather than God's. It was my security. God has been teaching me and helping me. Thank God for the opportunity He gave us there. By His grace much has been accomplished. He gave us a good home and made us happy together and with our children. The training and experience He afforded me is needed elsewhere. In a crucial hour like this I must not lean back and rest on my oars. If others can carry on there for the present—and possibly do what I haven't been able to do, well and good. We are not our own. He who died to redeem us, lives to use us. You don't have to leave home. If you prefer to stay where you are, do so. Your happiness and well-being and that of the children means all to me. Naturally I get very lonely and homesick—but what of it—if I am where God wants me. I am naturally selfish and see so many things in which I should have been different. But thank God for His grace. He is still dealing with me. Now then, I must carry through. I want to enlist as many as possible in the central national program. My support is OK, but I want enough income to support Washington, D.C. leadership and the work elsewhere. This I believe is God's will. The work must be established in three major cities. Upon the termination of the war there will be many men available to carry on. Now the ground-work must be laid and our leadership brought to face God in humility, prayer and obedience.

Abraham Vereide at 19,
soon after his arrival in America.

Vereide at 40 years of age.

Vereide in 1950
at 63 years of age.

I wrote you yesterday that I would like to have you come East. Of course I would, but if you feel differently about it, act as God leads and makes His will evident.

God will bless and reward you. You have stood by heroically through several chapters. Each one meant a crisis and a new birth. But they all represented larger usefulness and progress. This is my last. It meant much to tackle the city, then the state, then planting the seed in California, B.C., and across the country. Now the work must become cohesive and a functioning fellowship and an army. Life and opportunity here thrills me.

Hotel Washington, Washington, D.C.

1-19-44

We had a wonderful retreat with House and Senate members tonight. God was there. God is surely at work. I am so thankful that He has called me and is using me in this manner influencing the whole nation, yes, affairs of the world. Had an hour with Lord Halifax yesterday. He committed himself to go all the way with me in this program and especially for the International Round Table.

So many friends and the most thrilling work. Senator Wiley remarked to a group—that mine was the biggest work he knew of. It is all of God. I certainly don't deserve this privilege. But it is grace and more grace.

Hotel Washington, Washington, D.C.

1-22-44

Things are moving so rapidly now. I wish that I could stay, for it is getting so interesting. I came back from the Capitol this afternoon shouting happy. Praise God for His leading and blessing. Had breakfast here with Congressman Hays who was elected chairman of the House Group. He is a wonderful fellow. My choice. Deeply spiritual, sound, intellectual and a real leader in Congress. We planned the program and set it up. Then we met with the rest of the executive committee at 12 and went over the whole program and details. We had a period of prayer and dedication and I sort of installed them for their jobs. Dr. Judd of Minnesota, Vice-Chairman, and Poulson of Los Angeles, Secretary, etc.—men of highest caliber. Now that group is going to go forward as a real power for God in U.S. Congress. I am happy and released as the result, for I have carried it as a burden and unfinished responsibility. Meeting regularly all right, but it wasn't the right leadership. At 10 A.M. I met with the Senate Committee. They too adopted in total my program and elected the committee, etc.

Hotel Washington, Washington, D.C.

1-24-44

This has been an effective day spiritually. Breakfast Group in the hotel at 7:45 a.m.—meetings on the Hill at 9:30, 10 and 10:30. A very full day tomorrow. Just 2½ days more and so much to accomplish. Thank God for grace and strength.

Mattie—I show your pictures and tell about you and the children. I am proud of you. I do love you.

Hotel Washington, Washington, D.C.

1-25-44

This is Wednesday and I have concluded my work on the Hill—nearly. It was a good meeting and well attended in the Senate. I had a chance to unload. Then a conference with a few of them—then to the House with meeting—then back to Senate for some interviews and now 12 noon and back to my room with a sense of let down. Now I just want dear Mattie, to rest and relax with you. I can pray and weep and then feel better.

Yesterday I had lunch with Dr. Peter Marshall of the New York Avenue Presbyterian Church. We have become close friends.

Now I must pack and get ready as the morrow is filled with engagements. Have some socks to mend. I walk much and it is hard on socks. Leave 4 *P.M.* for New York.

Hotel Statler, Boston

1-29-44

Thursday in Washington and yesterday in New York. It was a blessed conclusion in Washington with prayer meeting in my room and the work in rather good order. New York was full from start to 11:30 *P.M.* when I went to the train. Very profitable. J. C. Penney, of Penney Company took me to lunch at the Union League Club there. He is issuing an invitation to a retreat for key business executives to be held upon his return from the South. He took me to the oldest Protestant church in America—the Marble Collegiate on 5th Avenue and introduced me to the famous pastor, Dr. Peale. There we had prayer and good fellowship. Dr. P. will cooperate in the retreat with some of his men. Also called on Dr. Ayer, pastor of 1st Baptist who has 1500 out for prayer meeting the year around. They all had heard all about me and the work and were extremely cordial. Had oyster stew at the depot, too much, so I didn't sleep so well.

Thank God for all these opportunities. He gives the open door. He goes before me. He is with me. How very blessed to know! Night or day—east or west—I am always "in the bosom of the Father."

Absence from you and Jr. and Alicia and grandchildren is hard and I make a fuss about it, but other men in business and military life seem to take it as a matter of course.

The Breakfast Groups of Chicago

2-2-44

Well, step by step, the Lord leads. I have been in this building all day. Began at 9 and now it is 6 *P.M.* We had fine luncheon meeting. God did bless me. I have got the office arranged fairly well in this light corner room with four windows, two desks and typewriter desk and five chairs. Breakfast in the morning and luncheon with three of Chicago's industrial giants at the Union League Club. So each day has its opportunity and responsibility.

I went to the dentist yesterday upon my arrival. The dentist is on this floor, a member of the Breakfast Group. I am so thankful to have this dentist whom I have pointed to the Lord before and personally got him to the Breakfast Group—now he is here on this floor.

Hotel Book-Cadillac, Detroit, Michigan

2-5-44

Dr. Peter Marshall from Washington, D.C., will be Lenten speaker here for a week and I want to use him before a Breakfast Group.

Book-Cadillac Hotel, Detroit, Michigan

2-6-44

My work is very essential for victory to prepare and build the morale, the spirit, the faith and vision. It is also most important in preparing for peace. I know God has called me and is leading me on from day to day. I am now on the train bound for Chicago. The depot was crowded. Many crying saying farewell to boys leaving for the service. The long train is crowded.

Union League Club of Chicago

2-8-44

Had lunch today with the next president of U.S.A.—Honorable Congressman Dirksen. Well, some think so. I will vote for him if he is nominated.

Charles J. Frisbie to Abram:

2-9-44

I read with surprise—and with *pride*—when you resigned from the Seattle Breakfast Group to take up bigger work for the good of the nation. I am proud of you, Abram. Now your "light" is not "under a bushel" any more and a "big man" is going to lend his voice to God to do "big things". Abram, I'll never forget you and your *forceful* spiritual guidance. You have been my model of strength and fearlessness in Christ. I have been asked by my former commandant to be the liaison officer between Civil Air Lines and Naval Air Lines.

Union League Club of Chicago

2-10-44

How blessed it is to be surrendered to *His* plans, program and purpose! Our business is to mind *Him* and leave it there. The only time we can truly say "The *Lord* is my Shepherd" is when we are willing to be the sheep. The Shepherd must lead. I have the sense of utter security.

Next Wednesday I meet with fifteen top leaders of Chicago—Room 800 at the U.L. Club. At the center of this new move are: Nathaniel Leverone, president Canteen Company of America and twenty-five corporations; J. C. Cunningham, president Republic Flow Meter Company, a wonderful fine Christian man of St. Clair's type—Presbyterian; Roy Ingersoll—president Ingersoll Steel Corporation and Ross-Werner Corporation, a great industrialist, 25 plants; Hughston McBain—president Marshall Field Company; and George Haight, attorney, director and trustee of Chicago Milwaukee R.R. and president Union League Club. The possibilities are tremendous.

Union League Club of Chicago

2-13-44

Dr. Glenn Clark was in town yesterday. I didn't know it. But he had a meeting of some of Chicago's Religious leaders and, Mattie, I am humbled and rather amazed that he told those men that I was the outstanding religious leader in America today.

Don't say that to anybody. For it is not me—and further more it would be awful for me to think so.

The new letterhead used by Vereide—"The Breakfast Groups" of Chicago—2-16-44

Groups of men meeting every week for Christian fellowship and Bible study.

No partisan politics, denominationalism or financial appeals.

Union League Club of Chicago

Your letter just received. J.G. told me when I left that he wanted to help with the Washington expenses. My account was down, so I wired him to make a deposit and wrote him later. I'm sorry, deeply sorry, that this has caused him ill feeling and reported it to you that way. My support is surely forthcoming. I have received some, but it has taken time to get things underway with all the other work I have had. Please Mattie, trust me and God to work it out, and be of good cheer. Under the blessings of God, we are going to be firmly established.

Nothing great is easily won. Friday morning—I didn't mail this yesterday. The incident brought much reflection and prayer. I asked God to search me and try me, to speak to me. If I am wrong or pursuing a wrong course to show me—prayer, tears and humbling before God. But the voice was, "Be faithful—carry through, I am with you." I can take anything when I know that I am where *He* wants me. I am not bound to succeed, but I am bound to be true. I am not bound to win, but I am bound to live up to what light I have.

Union League Club of Chicago

4-12-44

[Vereide visits the city he first came to as an immigrant.]

At Butte several of the men came down to meet me. They were full of ideas and enthusiasm. Things are really moving ahead there. I was much encouraged by seeing them and hearing their report.

Union League Club of Chicago

4-13-44

The Breakfast this morning was spiritually rich and challenging. There was especially one man leagues ahead of me in his quiet trust in God. My, how God was working through him! That's the way I want to be. The noon meeting was also very good. The committee afterwards was most gratifying. They as the National Executive Committee would be responsible for budget and business. They were very considerate and interested.

Union League Club of Chicago

4-17-44

Your letter last night made me blue. I was ready to throw up the sponge, quit all and go home and take a job of some menial type. I just turn the business over to God, that He either heal you or else send me back home.

This morning he gave me the assurance of victory—first, that you would be all right; second, that I am to do what *He* tells me. Love Him supremely and trust and obey. His ways are higher than our ways. Third, that salary and adequate funds beyond anything in the past would be forthcoming.

These words come also—"He that loveth father or mother or wife more than me is not worthy of me." He who was God became man and died for me on the cross. Nothing is too much for me to give for Him.

Oh yes, I have been disobedient and made many blunders, and many times I have said that I am not worthy of a good woman like you. But by His grace, He has led me along and thank God, I know I am saved, I do belong to Him, with *all* I am and have. Here is a mission among our nation's leaders. God called me. He has used me. I must carry on till *He* guides otherwise. Mattie, *His* will and plan is best for both of us. Mattie, dear, please be of good cheer. I do love you so much and will be always your true and devoted Abram. Just now relax, trust Him who died to save you, trust Him to heal, guide and keep you!

University Club, Washington, D.C.

4-25-44

Well, here I am in busy Washington, D.C. The speaker at the American Banker's Convention said that there was not much hope for the future for our country except as our leaders were led by God. Faith and fortitude are essential. The hope he said was in the multiplication of smaller groups like the Breakfast Groups. Great openings are before me here both in Congress and government departments and life at large. I am glad that this is God's business and I am His agent.

University Club, Washington, D.C.

4-25-44

Capon Springs is an old historic place, the oldest building about 200 years—back in the West Virginia Mountains against a national forest. The famous springs water is healthgiving. We had marvelous food in great abundance—all produced on the 1000 acre farm. I played golf, climbed mountains, walked and prayed with men daily out or in. It was a time of victory. Conducted breakfast group meetings and instructed men in how to do it. We were on our knees in prayer and had God's touch.

Seventeen-Twelve Walnut Street, Philadelphia, Pa.

5-2-44

My, how good to hear your voice last night and that of Junior. I was really very homesick, and therefore selfish in spending $3.00 for the call, but it was worth it, for I was greatly comforted. However, if it is disturbing to you, please let me know and I will forego the pleasure. The meeting I addressed last night at Calvary Baptist Church in New York was largely attended and blessed of God.

Then we had morning breakfast, forenoon conferences and luncheon at the Waldorf Astoria Hotel, afterwards eight men to the room of Harvey Hill for prayer and planning. Then at 3 *P.M.* another meeting. 6:30 another, 7:30 another, 8:30 another and by 12 o'clock I was tuckered out.

The Consolvo Hotels, Richmond, Va.

5-2-44

The M's are out tonight, so their 10-year-old son Frederick and I had dinner together. The Negro maid prepared a simple dinner. This boy is very hard to manage. The parents don't know how to handle him. He told me his story and I told him mine, how I accepted Jesus Christ into my life as a little fellow and how He has been with me up through the years. Then he too accepted Jesus and prayed. Afterwards he came and thanked me. He has been a model boy tonight. I helped him some with his school work too. Now I must dig in with some of my work.

The Army and Navy Club, Washington

5-6-44

Yesterday I was in the most elaborate and beautiful home ever. The grounds, flowers, trees, setting and the magnificent interior! It was former Ambassador to Moscow, Joseph E. Davies. I had a long visit with him. All that splendor didn't move me. A humble home and godly folk appeal to me much more.

At 9 *a.m.* here, 6 *a.m.* there, a group of praying women will be praying for you and your complete recovery. Relax, trust and rejoice in God! Remember you are *His*. Your body is His. He indwells, restores and reigns. Disregard symptoms. Believe God.

Some days I am much troubled and tempted to doubt. Sometimes the devil tries to get me to doubt God, the Bible and all, especially when I am tired. I am ineffective when I doubt. He knows it. But then if I can rest, pray, read my Bible or just simply rest, God comes in sweet reassurance again. Mattie, I know He lives, loves and you are His very own.

LETTERS REVEAL THE MAN

Civic Education Service, Washington, D.C.

5-10-44

Last night I worked till late and couldn't sleep much. Thinking about the Senate meeting this morning and all my work. I should have cast my burden on the Lord—"commit thy way unto the Lord, trust also in Him and He shall bring it to pass"—but I carried it. So I am tired today and less effective. God is so merciful—He sustains and helps us in our infirmities. He has led and given wisdom, grace and strength for another day.

I wept and prayed for you this afternoon after reading your letter —that you were not any better. I wanted so much to just leave for home. Then a voice seemed to say, "Don't weaken, trust God and carry through." I wonder if you didn't experience relief, His gracious touch?

I had lunch with Dr. Marshall yesterday. We have become rather chummy. He is a man after my own heart. Senators Wherry of Nebraska and Gutry of N. Dakota had me for lunch today and then a meeting with several. I do believe God is using me and gradually working out His purpose. He doesn't seem to be in such a hurry as I often am.

The Army Navy Club, Washington

5-11-44

Another letter today and you feeling some better. Thank God, we can surrender all! Rest in His will, for His will is always best—for with Him is *infinite love* and a glorious future. Always something better ahead. I am surprised that you still have that feeling about City Chapel. Really, I am so glad and thankful for the way God has led. My task and my future is so much larger, richer and better; I rejoice in my task. I look forward to a remarkably rich ministry. This morning the larger group in the House gave me a great recognition and encouragement.

The way things are unfolding here is also evidence of God's hand being over us and with us. Tonight I have dinner here at this Club. Admiral Freeman is sitting near me. We are waiting for the rest to come.

What a fine body of men they are! Thank God for them!

Union League Club of Chicago

6-2-44

As I paused to pray for you again, the still small voice said, "Why don't you trust me?" Surrender fully to me—children, home, security, past, present and future with an eternal "yes"—to all the will of God. To rescue the perishing, to win men and women for Christ—without which they are lost—that's the all important thing. We are a team. You are working from the home angle. But we are all of one accord—united in and for Jesus Christ—our Saviour and Lord. It is His will, His program and cause. I pray and listen and obey. I have put my hand to the plough to go through that so many neglected and needy of our leadership and through them down the line—may be won for Christ.

Hotel Cleveland, Cleveland, Ohio

6-11-44

The two meetings with Admiral Freeman were indeed worthwhile. He is a prince.

National Committee for Christian Leadership

6-14-44

Board of Directors: (partial)
  Vice Admiral C. S. Freeman
    U.S. Navy (Retired)
    New York
  Congressman Walter H. Judd
    Minnesota
  Congressman John J. Sparkman
    Alabama
  Senator Raymond E. Willis
    Indiana
  Congressman Brooks Hays
    Arkansas
  David Lawrence, Publisher
    United States News
    Washington, D. C.
  Senator Alexander Wiley
    Wisconsin

The Robt. Morris Hotel, Philadelphia, Pa.

Lots of people will be coming there during the next few days for the Republican National Convention, to nominate president and vice president on the Republican ticket. We have an important breakfast meeting for them on the 27th.

They tell me that this work God has given me is bearing fruit and that these groups are wielding a great influence in our national life. Thank God a few men are won for Christ and really converted to a new life with repentance toward God and faith in the Lord Jesus Christ. This is the all important thing.

Hotel Cleveland, Cleveland, Ohio

6-17-44

God is working here in a mighty way. One man came clean through this afternoon. I am taken up from early till late—after 12 o'clock last night. Men are eager, hungry and responsive.

Union League Club of Chicago

6-18-44

The most blessed and fruitful retreat conference ever held. There were several outstanding conversions. My, what a time. Back on the train God used me to deal with a doctor—M.D., head of the State of Illinois hospitals, largely mental and psychiatric institutions.

In April 1945, came the devastating news that stunned the world, of President Roosevelt's sudden death. The gravity of the hour was a challenge to the spiritual morale of the nation's leaders. A memorable meeting took place on April 16th at Marian Johnson's home, and over ninety persons crowded into the big drawing room, some sitting on the floor, to hear messages from Senator H. Alexander Smith, Senator Lister Hill, and David Lawrence of the United States News and World Report. "It was an evening of challenge, preparation and dedication before San Francisco," Abram said.

The San Francisco conference for the formation of the United Nations Organization was about to start. Members of the U. S. delegation had suggested to Vereide that he should form from the representatives of the various nations a "spiritual United Nations" who would seek God's guidance and will in the proceedings. He held some preparatory meetings with members of the Senate Foreign Relations Committee and the Foreign Affairs Committee of the House of Representatives and with some from other governments, and then flew to San Francisco to attend the great gathering.

"We had several meetings," he wrote, "some smaller ones, and a dinner meeting which lasted over four hours at the St. Francis Hotel. Forty-six delegates came, the Mayor of San Francisco presided, and men from many nations spoke. The question was—the basis for unity, stability and progress for the United Nations. Before the evening was over, men had discovered each other on a new level, men who believed in

God in the first general category, then men who believed in Jesus Christ and the coming of His kingdom, and men who believed the Bible, the moral code, the fundamental laws of the whole superstructure of society, men who prayed. The basic, eternal truths of other religions being largely summarized in the teachings of Christ and exemplified by Him, the conclusion of many was that 'no man can lay any other foundation than that which is laid, even Jesus Christ.' "

Marian Johnson's rented home was sold suddenly, late in 1945, while the family was away. What provision would the Lord now make both for her own household and for I.C.L. activities? The house she had seen before, near Sheridan Circle, had seemed just the thing, and she had decided that would be the place, if they had the money to move and buy. Abram, meanwhile, and unknown to her, had been in touch with another agent, who had shown him the same house, 2324 Massachusetts Avenue. This was so exactly what they needed that he took it—by faith. In his journal in December 1944, he records, "Your prayer is heard. The house is yours—for the Lord. Thank You." They then discovered that they had both been led to the same place!

To acquire it as the property of I.C.L., a Fellowship Foundation was incorporated, and through an unusual set of circumstances, God provided the exact amount eventually needed to complete the purchase. I.C.L. had its Board of Directors spread over the country, under the chairmanship of Nathaniel Leverone, though it was then still using the earlier title of N.C.C.L. They authorized a small group of more permanent Washington residents to assume the local responsibility. The house had been a former legation. "It was the dream of a headquarters at our nation's capital come true," wrote Abram. "It was in answer to prayer. A four story building with two additional lots located on Embassy Row, facing Sheridan Circle and Massachusetts Avenue. The delightful garden at the back of the house overlooks Rock Creek Park. Right across this beautiful narrow gorge is Dumbarton Oaks of historic significance, with its gardens and surrounding terrain."

The Washington office was moved from 744 Jackson Place to the new headquarters. "We made our residence on the fourth floor. The offices are on the ground floor adjoining the main kitchen and a four-car garage. The next floor has the reception hall, the drawing room and library where smaller and larger gatherings are frequently held, a commodious, delightful dining room, a room for serving, the small kitchen and pantry. The rear room is a dining room for personnel or breakfast; the back porch is the popular eating place during the hot summer months. My office is on the third floor, where also are guest rooms and a business office for Fellowship House."

14 | HOW DOES HE DO IT?

How does Abram Vereide, the Norwegian immigrant, reach the hearts and win the confidence of the top men of a nation? By the simplest methods in all the world—by faith, love, and boldness.

Abram loves men. He expresses that love by thinking the best of men. Thinking the best of men, he takes it for granted that these who hold great responsibilities will both be seeking the highest and know their own need of power and wisdom beyond themselves to attain it. In other words, he is positive in his outlook. He knows all men are sinners, of course, but he also knows that to make that bald statement would not be effective with men in high places, successful, important, intelligent, powerful. There is something else that he is equally sure of—that no man can be at rest until he finds his rest in God. He therefore assumes that men want God, though they may not know it themselves.

A love of that kind is bold, and great boldness is an outstanding quality of the Holy Spirit in Abram, as in the apostle Paul. Boldness, simplicity, self-forgetfulness. Armed with these potent weapons, he has gone in where nearly everybody else would fear to tread. No approach in the love of God is stereotyped, and a verbal description of an "average" method can easily give the idea of a technique rather than the living vital I-Thou touch of man with man. Still less should anyone think it should be imitated.

Suffice to say that a man who comes with a Bible under his arm or with undue piousness would be discounted. Vereide has had to learn to appear as human and natural as any of the rest; but he always carries his ammunition with him—the New Testament in his hip pocket. However, he does not take it out where it isn't called for. His line of approach would often be to congratulate a man on his high office, to remind him how people across the nation are looking to him, and to inquire whether he is God's man, and if not, how can he function properly and make such important decisions without God? Then, "Don't you want to be God's man?" As he himself puts it: "My purpose is to bridge the gap between a man on his operating level and his becoming what he ought to be. These successful men don't have a need like the man in the street, but this is a means of showing them their need."

Congressmen have often said how little they realized what it would mean when Vereide first called on them. They would ask how much he wanted, or what pressure group was he with; and his answer would be that he had just come to invite them to a breakfast to talk to them about spiritual things. There are those who resent it and wish to see the back of him. Was the Gospel ever popular, in whatever form it is presented? But the amazing phenomenon of this country, and maybe to some extent of other countries today, is the change of climate towards religion, the willingness to listen and respond: the numbers who do respond to I.C.L. Breakfast Groups and other gatherings is evidence of the general welcome Vereide receives. There are congressmen who with tears in their eyes say, "Thank you, thank you, you are the first man to challenge me like this." As Senator Flanders of New Hampshire said, "Whenever Abram drops into my office, I drop everything and expect a message from the Lord." Senator Willis Robertson of Virginia said that, having served in the Congress for twenty-two years, "of all my experiences here I regard my attendance at the meetings of the Senate Breakfast Group the most interesting and the most valuable."

But it must not be thought an easy thing even to reach the presence of these men in high government positions. They often have to protect themselves from the time-wasters by a battery of secretaries. Today Abram is so well-known and respected by the nation's legislators that he can probably reach most that he wants to; but it was certainly not so when he started. He had to pray his way through from secretary to secretary.

Calling on a senator, the friend who was with Abram gives this description of the brief contact: "I was with him in the Senate building, when he walked into a senator's office, sat down, and invited him to the breakfast group. He only took five or ten minutes, and before he left, he put his arm around him and started to pray." Abram has the simple habit on all occasions of passing from conversation to prayer, without announcing it, and in the most natural way—merely changing from talking to a man to talking to God. He is talking with you, and before you know where you are, you are praying!

But it would be misleading to leave the impression that Vereide's boldness and persistency could better be named tactlessness. Of all men he is God's salesman, God's diplomat. With only a look at him, one can recognize a man whom the Spirit has molded into God's ambassador—dignity without any air of superiority, the equal in outward appearance of any among whom he moves, poise yet with the warmth, humility and freedom of true brotherliness. See him at a dinner table with a group of important men, political leaders, military men, lawyers, business executives. He gets them talking, asking them questions about problems in government, and lets them talk it out. They express viewpoints with which he may totally disagree and feel need setting right; but they are so intelligent, he could not touch their fields. But when they stop, he begins, for he knows something they don't know, and by the time they have talked it out, they find what they don't know. Others would dash in and preach, or get worrying lest they would lose their chance; but Abram has learned to relax and wait for God. "What is the greatest discovery you have made?" is a question he will sometimes ask, picking the right men to ask and getting them to open up. He uses questions more than an expression of his own opinion. "Dad's highlight," as his daughter Alicia says, "is not in a great cathedral, but round the table. These men who are important recognize reality. Dad has this quality of humility these men recognize. He does not blow a trumpet as some men do when they speak to senators and are trying to impress them. He is always trying to push the other man forward, and is himself never anything but that poor boy from Norway who knew the Lord."

"I saw that selfless directness recently," she continued, "when I was going with Dad towards the swing doors of the Du Pont Circle Building where we now have our offices. We saw a grand car draw up at the building, with some notables in it in colored robes. We wanted to know who they were. I was about to ask the chauffeur. Dad went up to the men themselves and asked if they had come to see him! He found they were ministers of state for Nigeria, who have an office in the same building. They were Christians, but through the seven days they had been in the city had only attended cocktail parties. Dad asked them to a breakfast group next morning. They came and were so grateful for the Christian contacts."

On another occasion he was a guest at the Vietnamese Embassy. Men from the embassies of Korea, Indonesia, and others were present. They had cocktails, then dinner. Abram told his host that he had to leave early, but asked permission to say a few words before doing so. He started by saying how glad he was to be with them, then continued, "I would like to leave three words with you—faith, hope, love. You have faith in your country, you have hope for your country, and love—how we need love. Oh, to love the whole world." Then he told in a word how his experience in Norway had changed his life, how Christ had changed him. People had put down their glasses and were getting uneasy. But there he stopped. He gave them faith, hope, love. "It was a masterpiece," said Alicia. "A smile and advice. We would have added, You should believe this. But this was God's diplomat."

Taxi drivers, porters on trains, the men who shined his shoes, bellhops in the hotels, men at gas stations or airports are as much those for whom Christ died as senators and congressmen. To each he speaks, and often puts his arm around them and prays for them. Sometimes it is prayer in reverse! He arrived at one hotel so sick that he asked the bellhop who took him to his room if he were a Christian. On hearing that he was, he asked him to pray for him, and they knelt together by the bedside, the bellhop praying for the hotel guest.

In a taxicab one day he asked the driver, "What is the good

news today?" "Oh," he replied, "there is no such thing as good news. At home and abroad it is all dark and hopeless. Do you have any good news?" "Yes," answered Vereide, "and I am bubbling over to tell it." "What is it?" "God is. He is love with a purpose, a plan and a program for the world and for you and me. His love is revealed in His plan of redemption through His Son Jesus Christ. He came to seek and to save fellows like you and me, and to make us what we ought to be." "Well," the driver remarked, "that is the news that needs to be told. But how can we get it out?" "It is very simple," Abram told him. "It begins with you and me. We believe it, accept it, act on it, and then tell it to the one next to us." The driver paused awhile and said, "You've got it. Let's do it." And every now and then in Abram's journal, there is the note at the bottom of the page for that day, "A man accepted Christ today."

Even while the author was talking to Abram about the writing of this book, the phone rang. On his return to the table, he said to his wife, "That was Mrs. Beaudray from Chicago. She phoned to say that yesterday her husband, when coming out of his place of business, looked up to heaven, exclaimed, 'Jesus Christ!' and fell dead." She wanted to know if Abram would come up to conduct the funeral. Then he turned to me and said, "How glad I am that a few years ago I was traveling in a car with that man, and spoke to him of the Saviour. We stopped the car while we prayed and he accepted Him. Both he and his wife have remained my close friends ever since. Thank God he went with the name of Christ on his lips."

15 | CRISIS

Sudden, severe illness nearly ended Vereide's life in 1946. While on a speaking tour in the Middle West, he was taken ill when speaking in St. Paul, hospitalized in Minneapolis, and operated on for a ruptured appendix. But it was also a meeting place with God. "It was in this hospital," he wrote, "when the doctors and nurses concluded that I was about to go and 'shake hands with St. Peter,' that a new spiritual discovery came to me. First, there was the sense of absolute security and lack of any fear. Before going to the operating table, I wrote a note to my wife and children, conveying this to them for their own sake as well as for mine. It was an indescribable reality and a factual relationship in an hour like that.

"Sometime after the operation, I had such a vivid communion with God that I seemed to leave the body. I could see my body there in bed, but I was caught up into an ineffable glory of divine reality, which has given me an ineradicable sense of certainty that the personality is independent of the body; the body is our means of contact with the physical world, but mind, will, imagination, with all the consciousness of being and characteristics of the entity of a person, exist apart from the body. Jesus was more real than human beings about me, and so constantly so during those trying days of weakness, that I was continually saying, 'Thank you, Jesus.'

"A few weeks stay in a modern hospital gives one a keen sense of one's indebtedness to the medical and nursing profession, the dedicated personalities, coupled with the application of modern discoveries in medicine and surgery. I owe a very special debt of gratitude to the great skill of my surgeon, Dr. Henry Lee, and to the Norwegian Christian nurse, Edna Larsen, who cared for me with such devotion.

"It is also an opportunity to discover the healing benefit of the loving attention and prayers of loved ones and friends, more numerous than one realized.

"The power of persistent, believing prayer as the turning-point during those first five days of crisis became self-evident. My wife and daughter were soon at my bedside, and the latter read to me from the Bible on her knees. Others at Fellowship House and elsewhere kept touch by telephone and held me up before God. Humanly, the odds were against my recovery, but slowly the condition changed and my strength gradually returned as the life of God was poured into me. When human beings offer themselves as channels, great is the power of healing prayer.

"My oldest son, Warren, was still in the service of the state of Washington; but our second son, Milton, who upon his graduation from the University of Washington had enlisted in the Service and after four years in the North Pacific theater had returned to civilian life and entered business in Seattle, hastened to my bedside. He looked after me and refused to leave until he had brought me safely back to our home in Washington, D.C., where our youngest son, Abe Jr., was anxiously awaiting my safe return. We gave thanks to God for His great goodness.

"One day Milton came to me with this proposition. 'Dad, I believe you ought to take a few months away to recuperate and visit your old home in Norway. You cannot go alone, but if you go, I will go with you and pay my own expenses.'

"General Hilldring of the U. S. Department of State had discussed with me some time earlier a plan of my visiting Germany to discover potential leadership with whom we might cooperate as far as the American Zone was concerned. Other invitations had come to me from other countries in connection with our program of Christian Leadership. Now it seemed this was a confirmation of the visit."

It was to be more than a time of recuperation, therefore. It was to be God's time, as Abram recognized, for the establishment of the I.C.L. on an international level.

"We had the great joy of meeting with church, education, labor, business and government leaders of Norway," reported Vereide, "and to be invited to the Palace for a delightful visit with King Haakan and Prince Olaf, and to learn how the protecting hand of God had been over them and His guiding hand with them and the people during the war. I gained ten pounds in ten days during my stay with my sisters and relatives in Nordfjord, Every house had a flag up for us. It was a feast beyond words for body, mind and spirit, to be in their midst. It was a relationship, not only physical, but profoundly spiritual."

In his personal letters to his wife, he gave the family touch:

I am sitting at the old family table in the little cottage of my childhood. Over in the corner is the bed where I was born and which, after mother's death in 1892, was occupied by father and me. The pictures on the wall, the books

in the old bookcase are—many of them—of the long ago
and old friends. What sacred memories! Now the house is
unoccupied. It is standing on ground belonging to the
State, and they are unwilling to sell. The Community want
to retain it for special smaller gatherings. It is indescribable—what I see, sense and the emotions that grip me.
The fruit trees, berry bushes, the rocks and the babbling
brook seem to understand me and love me back. The
hills, woods, the big old trees—recall adventures of my
childhood. The mountains spotted with snow banks,
green fields, heather, woods or jagged dark cliffs, dec-
orated with white streams or dashing, thunderous water-
falls, speak the mighty language of the ages and remind
me of the passage God gave me when I left here March
1905, 41 years ago—Isaiah 54:10—My sisters, Karen and
Eli, their families, relatives and friends are all in festive
attire overjoyed at our coming home. We feast on all the
good things here such as goat cheese, dried mutton and
pork, Rummerkoole, Rommepot, Waffles, etc.—4 meals a
day. It was wonderful to visit the graves of father, mother,
and my two sisters, Inger and Anna. Yesterday I preached
to a large audience in the old State Church where I was
baptized and confirmed. Many relatives came home to
Eli's for dinner and late afternoon coffee—which is a
real meal. It was a great afternoon with prayer, testimonies and talks about former days and the present, how my
sisters had started the Sunday school work, missionary
enterprises, etc. here and how God had led forward. Many
transformed homes and individuals. It is really marvelous
what God has wrought, and I had the joy of leading some
of the relatives to Christ.

The communities of Lote made our visit a half holiday.
At every house the flag was up, and young and old came
with their baskets of food to spend the afternoon and early
evening to hear the Word of God and this man from America. We went to Oslo for conferences there. Leadership
groups of government, business and various professions
afforded us the opportunity to convey our message and
to learn from them. The king was a delightful fellow,
stately but humble, revealing inner release and a manly

grasp of the affairs of the nation. He is greatly loved and trusted over the whole country. The meeting with spiritual leaders of Oslo and other places was encouraging. Norway is rising again strong and resolute. They have much to teach us. Their Breakfast Group in Parliament is a vigorous body.

The visit continued to Sweden and Denmark, followed by "the joy of inaugurating breakfast groups of the Christian Leadership program in Switzerland." Then to Germany, where they were brought by General McNarney's private plane from Frankfurt to Berlin. "We were given every opportunity to acquaint ourselves with the operations of our own military government, the problems confronted, the plans prepared, the men in charge, and then to get around in the various zones, including the Russian, to see life among the people and visit with many German leaders."

He wrote to his wife:
"Here we are in Berlin! How strange! Met with suffering Christians who wept with us. What an experience to be with them! Lunch with members of the general staff and spoke this evening to about 150 military leaders. Meet with German church leaders tomorrow, General Clay and Governor Sewell. The results in permanent connections and leadership for the Br. Groups has already made our trip worthwhile in Germany, with Dr. Otto Fricke of Frankfurt as chairman."

This tour resulted in the work of I.C.L. being organized internationally in January 1947, under the larger title of the International Council for Christian Leadership (I.C.C.L.). The existence of both an I.C.L. (national) and I.C.C.L. (international) is confusing for the average person, so, to set the record straight, it is better that we stick to the one simple title of I.C.L. (International Christian Leadership), in all our references to the movement, even if it is technically inaccurate when referring to its international activities.

As Abram flew home, he wrote:
What a thrill to fly! Particularly on a beautiful clear night with the stars above and wide horizon over cities,

mountains and country communities. The thousands in cottage and palace, humble and rich, but all of the great human family for whom Jesus went to Gethsemane and Calvary. Here I sit reflecting and worshiping God. I do love Him and praise Him. We really only understand as we love. For *love is the capacity to understand.* Oh, for the fullness of God's great redeeming love that we may understand and redemptively help all people!"

That same year he was invited to visit Paris at the time of the Peace Conference, where he conducted daily prayer meetings in Senator Vandenberg's apartment. An international conference was held in Zurich, Switzerland, and others in Holland and England. Delegations visited a large number of countries "to foster Christian leadership, religious liberty, and vital Christianity."

In the summer of 1946 a series of weekend I.C.L. conferences also began at Aymar and Marian Johnson's former home, Woodland, at Islip, Long Island. The latter now lived on another part of the property, the old family house being sold to the Hewlett School for Girls; but it was kindly made available during the summer months. These conferences continued through several years, with Abram leading and occasionally Bob Doing, and Marian Johnson or Alicia Abrahamsen running the household. Up to fifty would attend. Several weekends were held for members of the United Nations, through the assistance of Donald Stone. On another memorable occasion, Dr. Karlis Leyasmeyer of Latvia gave such a tremendous message on Christ and Communism, having himself escaped a communist firing squad, that he has been occupied ever since lecturing on college campuses throughout the country and to men's groups such as Rotary and Kiwanis under the auspices of I.C.L.

At these various conferences Vereide again defined the purpose of I.C.L. and the Breakfast Groups. "One world in active cooperation in commerce, science, labor, and education should be one world in spiritual unity and moral convictions. There is only one Book for the whole world—the Bible. There is one central Personality for all ages, all races and all people, the only One in whose life there is no discrepancy, in whose character there is no flaw, demanding universal obedience because of who He is, what He is, and what He has to bring. He is King of kings, the Prince of peace; He is the eternal Son of God and Saviour of the world. He is Jesus, the Christ.

"Jesus started the first Breakfast Group. In chapter 21 of the gospel of John the story is recorded. A group of men in the fishing business met Jesus early in the morning. So we take the hint; we meet Him early, we begin the day with Him.

"He instructed them; we receive guidance from Him in how to do business. He invited them to breakfast. He had a fire where they could warm themselves; He had fish and bread ready for them, and He suggested that they bring some of their own catch as well!

"Then Jesus began to talk to them. He asked the leader of the group, Simon Peter, the searching question, 'Simon, do you love me more than these?' (the fish and fishing business). He answered in the affirmative. 'If you do, do something about it; express it—feed my sheep.' His orthodoxy was basically his faith in and devotion to Jesus Christ. The test of his relationship was his love for Jesus expressed in service to human need among children, youth, and maturity, providing their need physically, socially and spiritually. And the final instruction to him was, 'Follow Me.'

"As we review nearly 2000 years of history since this beginning, we observe that as men have stuck together in this fellowship with Jesus and put first things first, vital leadership has been produced and maintained. The small group is usually more effective.

"At the center of every group there is a small core of one or more committed men through whom the Spirit of God works in guiding the group along. Every vital group is a recruiting group. They are constantly on the job to win others to the Way. The principle is to translate the truth into life and action, and to discover and demonstrate in every area 'the better way.' It is not a matter of imposing ourselves on others, whether in the United Nations or among other religions, but it is in joyous freedom and disciplined earnestness, to be practical exhibits of the way that works, the way of the ultimate.

"There is no city or community that does not need a group of this type, where every department of life, from government, business, industry, labor and education, can sit down together once a week and compare notes, check their operations with the divine blueprint, and invoke the guidance and blessing of God as they seek His solution to current problems.

"Our church rolls are loaded with dead timber. Church membership is frequently a handicap, because it represents a privilege which is a neglected responsibility. Men are lost in the crowd and immunized from the real thing by a mild dose of nominal Christianity.

"It is frequently a matter of visiting men in their own offices and talking with them face to face in a language they can understand. Then as men yield to the wooing and awakening Spirit of God, something happens. You have got the beginning of a group.

"Every city is teeming with hungry, groping men who are desperately in need of God, and God in Christ, and Christ in their own lives. The simplicity of the start is often a stumbling block, for it takes all the courage and initiative a man can muster. A man who may be bold elsewhere is frequently a coward in this realm that matters most; but where men really begin to meet, regardless of their ignorance and detachment from the Source of life, if there is an open mind, a humble heart, and a determined perseverance, the truth from the Bible, the facts of life, the experience of others, and the illumination of the Holy Spirit will produce the transforming results.

"There is a striking statement in the fifty-ninth chapter of the Book of Isaiah, where a gloomy picture has been painted of conditions that prevailed. 'God saw that there was no man.' The man of the hour was lacking, the man who is not afraid of his future politically, the man whom money cannot buy, or praise or criticism spoil, the man who will be uncompromisingly true to his convictions, in love with men and with a vision and passion for the truth. Heaven is bending low to bless that man, and to keep and sustain him through thick and thin. That man is wanted today everywhere.

"The second statement in this passage of Scripture is, 'and God wondered that there was no intercessor,' there was no one to pray. And adequate leadership is raised up by God in answer to prayer. That is why I have been hunting out any humble person anywhere I have been, who knew how to pray, to get him to begin to pray for our leadership, and that God will raise up the men of His own choice." A key verse for I.C.L. groups is Acts 2:42, emphasizing the six requisites for a successful group: "And they continued [1] steadfastly [2] in the apostles' doctrine[3], and fellowship[4], and in breaking of bread[5], and in prayer[6]."

Two movements are plainly apparent in the church today—back to the layman, and back to the small group, the house-meeting. I.C.L. has been in the van of both these—essentially a layman's movement, and essentially a group movement. The church *is* the layman. Vereide has always seen that. He would agree with John Newton, the ex-master of a slave ship, converted and become a clergyman in London, who had a great influence on William Wilberforce, the liberator of the slaves. It is said that he urged Wilberforce "not to become a religious recluse, but to return to politics. Newton enabled him to see the vision of a public life given to God. Wilberforce must take back his new Christian experience and insights into that milieu to which both by birth and intellectual eminence he belonged." As Melvin Evans of Democracy in Action puts it: "It is a matter of blending the spiritual with the economic in proper proportions that lifts people out of their lethargy and makes them say, 'I am starting tomorrow morning on something totally new and different that will make me God's partner in this tremendous task.'"

16 | IN SENATE AND HOUSE

The Breakfast Groups in Senate and Congress have now been meeting without intermission for eighteen years. Week by week about ten to fifteen Senators and thirty to fifty Congressmen set aside that hour to listen to God. Busy as they are, would they come if it was some formal religious exercise? There is no glamor attached to it, no advertisement, no publicity. Its basis is privacy. None can attend except those for whom it is meant. One of their own members leads, the Scriptures are read, there is discussion, sharing of problems, prayer. The searchlight of God's Word is turned on motives and activities. Decisions which affect the nation are made subjects of prayer.

In 1945, the Hon. Paul B. Dague reported on the activities of the House Group: "The convening of the Second Session of the Eightieth Congress was marked by the resumption of the Thursday morning gatherings of the House Breakfast Group. The members, who meet each week, have been most positive in their declaration that out of these fellowship assemblies around God's breakfast table have come their greatest inspiration for coping with today's pressing problems. And almost universal among them is the conviction that more of God's mandates and the teachings of the Nazarene must be written into current legislation if we are to effectively work out a solution of the world's ills."

A senator opened the first meeting of the Senate group recently in a new session by saying that he was a fundamentalist and believed the Bible, and that when it says God opened the Red Sea for Israel, He did open it. Believing this, he took his special problem to the same God of Israel, and committing it to Him at nightfall, by the morning he had the answer. He could not say how, but he knew. One of the heads of the Foreign Affairs Department was there, and he stayed on at the meeting despite constant calls to the phone. It was a national crisis and he was seeking God's answer to a situation which occupied the headlines of the papers the next morning.

Mr. Christian Herter, former Secretary of State and a man of few words, came out of a meeting at the Statler Hotel. Seeing Vereide outside, he beckoned to him. "I want to tell you," he said, "how much I appreciate what you are doing. I don't come often but I want you to know that your work is much more far-reaching than you realize;" and he took Abram's hand and shook it warmly.

Senator Stuart Symington, one of the Presidential candidates for the 1960 election, said, "I want to give due credit to the Senate Prayer Group which meets each Wednesday morning. It has done more for me than anything else since I came to Washington." Senator Symington's faith had been destroyed at a university. He never attended church until he came to the Senate, where he found Christ through the Breakfast Groups. Senator Willis Robertson of Virginia wrote Vereide in 1955,

"As you know, I have served in the Congress now for 22 years, but of all my experiences here I regard my attendance at the meetings of the Senate Breakfast Group the most interesting and the most valuable."

Periodically there are special events. When Chief Justice Vinson of the United States Supreme Court was appointed by President Truman and confirmed by the Senate, Vereide asked him if he would like to join them in the Senate Breakfast Group for a period of dedication to his new position. "He said he would," writes Abram. "Attorney General Tom Clark came along. After the usual Scripture reading and comments and prayer with some comments from different men around the table, which is the custom, the Attorney General made his observations and gave his testimony, and then presented the Chief Justice, who told about his impressions from a Christian home, Sunday school, church, his own Christian convictions and personal faith in Christ. He emphasized the importance of the Bible being the Book of all the people and how the whole superstructure of government and jurisprudence is built upon it. Then the twenty-eight senators present from both parties joined hands for a moment of silent prayer, and Senator Forest Donnell of Missouri lead in the dedicatory prayer, invoking God's blessing on the Chief Justice, and dedicating him in the name of the Father, the Son, and the Holy Spirit to his exalted and important position."

The Chief Justice came up to Abram after the breakfast and remarked that he wished very deeply that it might have been broadcast to all the American people, for he felt that it would do more than anything else to restore the confidence of the people in their government and to unite the nation in a common faith."

In 1947 the *Christian Herald* published an article by a Jacob Simpson Payton, which was written to enlighten the public on these House and Senate Breakfast Groups. "The most durable thing on Capitol Hill," he wrote, "is the Christian religion. Skeptics who ask for evidence may find it in the weekly meetings of Senators and Representatives who comprise two 'Breakfast Groups,' links in a chain of coast to coast fellowship sponsored by the National Committee for Christian Leadership.

"During recent years Congress has been reorganized, party

control of the Legislative Branch has shifted. But ever since 1941, when by an act of faith Abraham Vereide proposed to a number of lawmakers that once a week they meet about the breakfast table for prayer, Bible study and exchange of views, the congressional Breakfast Groups have increased in attendance. Moreover, the numbers they attract refute the erroneous charge that religion is given scant consideration by members of Congress.

"No attempt is here made to burnish up tarnished reputations. Congress is but a microcosm of America. The good and the not-so-good may be found within its halls. A few may have ascended a ladder with one end planted in a notorious ward, but the majority of them had a Christian home for the first rung. And, by and large, they have resisted being processed into a state of spiritual dehydration under the withering effects of politics.

"Latest evidence of that resistance is seen in the Breakfast Groups—*and* in their response to Vereide. Just who and what in this man Vereide? . . . [Then followed a description of Abram in his earlier years] . . .

"It requires audacious faith to get even a good thing going in Washington, D.C. Every crackpot in America seems to arrive eventually in the Nation's Capital. To broach another meeting to congressmen when already they were complaining about impossible committee schedules might have seemed preposterous, but for two things. They were the persuasive manner in which Abraham Vereide laid upon the statute-makers' hearts their obligation to God—*and* their feeling of need, which is always the starting point of spiritual progress.

"There are many tables on Capitol Hill—tables about which committees frame legislation, or perfect it, or lay rejected measures like lifeless bodies on slabs in a morgue. But six years ago, Senators and Representatives drew up their chairs to two entirely different tables in the restaurants beneath the Capitol dome—there to partake of the Word which is the Bread of Life, and to discover how to expend the strength derived from personal righteousness.

"The congressional Breakfast Groups have always shunned publicity. Rightly or wrongly, they are adamant on the question of advertising their breakfast meetings. Politicians early

112

learn the danger of having their highest motives questioned or distorted. The Breakfast Groupers seem to fear—perhaps rightly—that unfriendly criticism will charge them with using their religion to strengthen their prestige, or of adopting it as a protective coloring.

"Among the earliest arrivals for the Breakfast Group meetings on Wednesday and Thursday mornings are Senators and Representatives whose names brilliantly illuminate the rosters of their political parties. While it might be an overstatement to say that 'the governing minds' of Congress attend, the attendance is entirely representative. And among them are old political 'wheel horses' who delight to be numbered with those who pull for God and Country.

"The first act upon arrival is for each member to hang up with his hat his partisanship, political armor and regional prejudices. In the place of Christian fellowship these 'Gentlemen of the Hill' meet on common ground. Removed from the noise and numbers of the clamorous world in which they move, they seek to hear the voice of God rather than that of *vox populi*. The welfare of America, always precious in their sight, becomes more so as its realization is interpreted by a member of the Group who, from their study of the Scriptures, know that national longevity, prosperity and happiness are conditioned by sound morality stemming from obedience to the divine laws.

"There is no time wasted on chatter over trivialities or political disputations. Members of the Breakfast Groups are deadly serious in their attempt to discover what is wrong with this feverish mass of humanity called the American citizenry, themselves included. They represent a wide variety of political complexions and convictions. Among them are left-wingers, middle-of-the-roaders, and reactionaries. Yet in the fellowship of searching for a better way to serve America, their differences are fused into a striking similarity. They become amazingly partisan: *they wish to be numbered on the Lord's side*.

"On the floors of Congress they may strive to howl and vote each other down over appropriations for defense, but in the Breakfast Groups they confess that America's security rests not so much upon supremacy in the air, on land or sea, as upon the supremacy in the heart of those qualities from which God builds and protects nations for durable and honorable service.

"On leaving a session of a Breakfast Group, these legislators often refer to it as their finest hour. Reference is not to any wisdom that they have imparted, but to the spiritual uplift they have received. The world, so impossible to view from Washington save through a murky, political mist, has appeared to them as from a window seat. Their vision has been clarified and their hopes strengthened. The open Bible on the breakfast table has proved a compass by which they may order their steps in the way of the Lord. In a world rocked by upheavals, they have glimpsed security in reliance upon the foundations 'of things that cannot be shaken.'

"Abraham Vereide's establishment on Capitol Hill of these Breakfast Groups has proved a work of immeasurable value. On Capitol Hill, where fame is fleeting and change is constant, there has been set apart an hour during which men entrusted with the responsibility of national leadership gather to study the blueprints which alone afford the pattern for the eternal in character and government.

"Congress has sometimes been called the home of lost causes. One cause, however, will never be lost on Capitol Hill so long as our legislators continue to rely upon the weaponry of prayer and Divine aid such as are made available at meetings of the Breakfast Groups."

17 | "A. V." AT HOME

"Good morning. Yes, this is Fellowship House, Very well, Sir, you may see me at 10:30." It was a call for an appointment. Again the phone rang. "Good morning, Sir. This is North 8766. How's that? Yes, this is the Headquarters of International Christian Leadership, sponsoring the Breakfast Groups throughout the country. I beg your pardon, what was that? Oh yes, regarding the Women's program. The Women's Auxiliary sponsoring prayer and Bible study groups represents a strong arm of this work throughout the nation and other parts of the world. Yes, the center of all these activities is Fellowship

House, located on Massachusetts Avenue by Sheridan Circle at the heart of Washington."

We are visiting with Abram Vereide and his staff at Fellowship House, getting an idea of how an average busy day is spent. He has been talking to people on the phone. Listen as he describes his activities. "It is 9:30 A.M., the mail has been opened, sorted and assigned for action. Some of the morning appointments have been taken care of, and now here we are in the lower office around a large table for a period of prayer and a brief Scripture meditation.

"It is 10 o'clock and each one to his task. Two men have arrived in the upper office to discuss some business matter. After they have presented their business and it has been taken care of, then it is my privilege to present mine. I also am in business and my business concerns them. They become interested and wonder what is up. I ask them frankly if they have enlisted in the great task of the program of the Kingdom. They inform me that they haven't, they have been so busy with their own affairs that the claims of Christ and the concern for others, the country and the world, has been beyond their scope of thinking. I tell them about God's great plan for man and His provision. They tell me about their own problems, and then the deeper needs in their own lives and the great blocks that hinder God from operating in and through us. I give them the story of redemption and then ask them if they would join me in a commitment of themselves to Christ, and accept God's great gift of forgiveness of sin, eternal life and inclusion in His family of co-workers with Him in the great Kingdom program. They say 'yes' and we go to prayer and to close the deal with God. Two groping, defeated men find the way to victory and to right relationships with God and men. We always leave a man's faith pinned on some Scripture verse, that he may not depend on feelings or on words of men, but always on what God says.

"By this time of the morning the ladies have been meeting various callers, and I usually ring for the secretary to come and get dictation. Through the generosity of two friends, a brand-new, up-to-date Audograph has been furnished, and it is my privilege to take the unanswered letters and begin my dictations. I am profoundly grateful for this time saving device. Here we have before us letters from Long Beach, Los Angeles, Portland, Seattle, Ontario, Baltimore, New York, Pittsburgh, Evansville, Hagerstown, London, Germany and Paris. We have an article for the News Letter to prepare.

"At the luncheon table today we had no one present except the staff. It was a happy fellowship, first about news and views, and then briefly about the work. Sometimes it is the meeting of the Board of Directors, some committee or representatives from the city, other parts of the country or from abroad. A group of ladies meets here, as part of the regular schedule, for an hour and a half during the morning on Thursdays for prayer and Bible study. Leadership of our nation, the work abroad, individual situations are always remembered at these gatherings.*

"Now a telephone call from an official of the Economic Co-operation Administration who wants an appointment for tonight. There are some problems in Europe to be talked over, he said, but most of all personal things and prayer. It is a joy when men are absolutely frank and openly tell the story and share their problems, and allow one the privilege of going to God in prayer together.

"My, what a happy privilege it was to talk over the matters of a Breakfast Group with a busy worker who had just called. So much has happened in his own life since he began to meet regularly with that body of men. He has also been instrumental in bringing others into the group and through the group back to the church and into the Kingdom. This man had found out what it meant to be saved and didn't hesitate to use the term. The question now was how to make the Group a vital, integrating factor in the city, a means to recruit men for Christ, to make representatives from the different departments of city life so practical in their Christian living that they would be translating the spirit, the principles and teachings of Jesus into daily life.

"At night we will have a meeting for spiritual fellowship, Bible study, prayer and the opportunity for everyone to give his report of progress, problems and work. This has been a day

*Recently new groups have been formed in Washington in The General Accounting Office, The Atomic Energy Commissioin, Labor and Management, and Administration Assistants.

of representation from this country only, while at other times we have people from many other nations.

"This is Fellowship House, a Christian Embassy, the head-quarters of this enterprise for Christian leadership that reaches out as a spiritual counterpart to the United Nations."

With that comes the comment in Abraham Vereide's journal, "Your job cannot be done by unconverted men. Rally the men who know God. Build firmly with men who are determined to know and do the will of God. Assign specific responsibility." A criticism commonly heard about I.C.L is that it is not definite enough. It has, they say, men attached to it or working for it who are not convinced Christians. There are sincere, orthodox believers who have pulled their skirts in from too close contact with I.C.L. on this account. But the position and calling of I.C.L. is crystal clear. Certainly, like the Saviour, its purpose is to mingle more with the unconvinced than the convinced. It is the genius of the Spirit in Abraham Vereide that he can move right in with men who are not noted as churchgoers, or who affirm a faith different from the evangelical Christian—the Roman Catholic or the Episcopalian, the Christian Scientist, the agnostic, or those of other religions. Such is his faith in the certainty of the Spirit speaking to all men, that he will sometimes ask such men to share in some I.C.L. activity, or on a sponsoring board, in the hope that, as they come closer into I.C.L. and mingle with its witnessing members, the deeper truth may be revealed to them; and certainly that has paid the dividends of the Spirit. There are many, whose faith was dim to say the least, or perhaps only nominal, who are today confirmed disciples.

An illustration of such criticism and Abram's reaction to it was when Frank Fuhr, assistant to Abram, and Gustav Gedat of Germany, arranged a meeting between him and Pastor Niemoeller. Niemoeller turned to Vereide and said, "I visited your groups and found men there drinking and smoking. On what grounds do you think you are international? What claim do you have to be leaders? I am even doubtful if you are Christian." (taking the name International Christian Leadership and taking it apart). "Niemoeller," says Fuhr, "was cold as ice and sharp as steel." "How would any normal man react to that?" asks Fuhr. "Abram looked at him—'That's a very interesting observation. Let's pray about it.' Abram bowed his head and we followed him. He prayed, Niemoeller moved and when we left, Niemoeller had his arm around A.V."

Wisdom is justified of all her children. So often the point in a man's character that seems most open to criticism is the particular quality in him that the Spirit can best use. If Vereide were not big, big in vision, big in an all-embracing love of men, big in reaching up to the world's big men as well as down to the small, big in bold outreach, big in faith in the Spirit's working in all men, big in following God's pattern no matter what others may say, big in claiming every aspect of man's activities of mind and body as well as spirit for the glory of God, there would be no I.C.L. A lesser man could never have been God's agent to the kind of people Abram reaches—the efforts of a lesser man would have boomeranged on him, and doors opened to Abram would have been fast shut to him. Thank God, the Spirit is original, and like the wind, bloweth where it listeth; "so is everyone who is born of the Spirit."

Letters to his wife during the one year of 1947 bear their own testimony:

Prince George Hotel, New York

2-3-47

Two years ago I received a letter of introduction from Howard Coonley to Mr. Charles Wilson, president of General Electric Co. I have not used it before today. We had 1½ hours with him. He is fully committed to the program.

On the train Saturday night, I sat down with two porters and talked about God, Jesus and redemption, life here and hereafter. Then we had a period of prayer.

Prince George Hotel

2-22-47

I enjoy dealing with men. It is my forte. To discover and mobilize, organize and vitalize, these represent our task. To be His instrument is the highest honor.

In Flight   Undated

High above the clouds and all is well. I have rested, read the evening paper, prayed for you all, and for the man next to me that I may win him for the Lord.

Hotel Californian, San Francisco, Cal.

5-16-47

Formed the NCCL and ICCL for Northern Calif. They adopted and accepted their quota of $2,500.00 for the NCCL and ICCL. Real commitment and enthusiasm. The chairman is Col. Leonard Worthington, whom I led to Christ several years ago. The treasurer is L. Koster, whom I also led to Christ years ago. He is head of the Bank of San Francisco—mission branch, so it is gratifying to reap the fruit of my labors in this manner.

The Barringer Hotels, Charlotte, N.C.

The president of the Federal Reserve Bank met me at the station and brought me to the hotel. He took me to the City Club to lunch with another banker and the president of a local college, then to inspect his bank, vaults, etc. God used me to lead the porter who brought my bags to the train to Christ, then the porter on the train, then two of the men at my table for breakfast, then the boy in the hotel, the maid and another fellow. It has been a great series. Some had backslid and needed renewal.

Traveling from Manchester to London, England

7-26-47

I have just led an engineer to Christ sitting next to me in this railroad car. We have had prayer. Now instructed him in how to start a group.

Zurich, Switzerland

8-4-47

Former Minister of Finance of the Hungarian Government—Dr. Fabinyi, has come through for the Lord and is a great help here, also a talented young Jew. God is working.

It was a special occasion when Abram was presented with the portrait of himself which hangs in the drawing room of Fellowship House. The place was packed and a senator, in making the presentation, was saying many flattering things. Abram was weak because of illness. He stood up, said no word, then took out his wallet and from it extracted a ticket. He read the printed statement on the ticket—"Void if detached." Pointing to the painting, he said, "And that man is no good if detached from Jesus Christ: he can only function if attached." And he sat down. That was typical of Abraham Vereide.

Abram and Mattie Vereide can look back on years of a marriage which has been a love match, a happy home, and a partnership in the Kingdom; this has been obvious in his letters to her. It was a union "in the Lord," and has had the Lord's blessing upon it. This book is necessarily centered on Abram and his calling, but behind Abram has always been Mattie, as all who come to Fellowship House well know. Because she is gracious, hospitable, hardworking, capable, and one in heart with her husband, Abram has not had domestic burdens to carry: he has always known that they were in safe hands. "What faithful and devoted service she is rendering daily!" he wrote about her in his journal in 1952. "She is not too proud to scrub and clean and do any kind of hard work. God will reward her some day. She has been faithful and good to me. God bless her!"

Though partly crippled now through a stroke, and only able to walk with difficulty, she can still be found cooking, serving meals, and entertaining her guests as though she were as able-bodied as ever.

The Vereides' oldest son, Warren, is Safety Engineer for the city of Seattle. He is active in the Breakfast Groups there and also as a Bible teacher in his own church.

Alicia Abrahamsen, their only daughter, became a widow in 1942; her two married children are on the West Coast, and the third is now assisting her in Washington. She herself joined her father and mother at Fellowship House fifteen years ago. Helping her mother in the household and hostess work, constantly in demand by phone and visitors for personal help, and increasingly sought for as a most gifted Bible teacher and public speaker, she is the most active part of the I.C.L. staff. Among the wives of the senators and congressmen and others, she is becoming something of what her father is to the men. She has started several prayer groups that meet regularly (one in the Library of Congress, another in the Pentagon) and groups for diplomats' wives, for newcomers, and for international contacts.

She was recently on a tour of I.C.L. meetings in Europe with a small team. Towards the end of the time she was joined by Marian Adair, the wife of Congressman E. Ross Adair from Indiana. In the course of their travels they were to visit Beatenburg, the beautiful little town perched up in the mountains over the Lake of Thun in Switzerland. The well-known Bible teacher and principal of a Bible School, Frau von Wasserzug, a Doctor of Philosophy, had invited Alicia to speak at the school. A somewhat humorous preparation was made for the visit, for thinking that her friend might feel a little out of place in such a dedicated atmosphere, Alicia advised her to remove some of her outward adornments—which she did in the car! But, whether that made any difference or not, she received during her stay at that school the inner adornment of Christ as Lord of her life. On their return to Washington, she became Alicia's teammate in starting meetings for the congressional wives, which have now become a regular part of the Fellowship House ministry. In the freshness of her new-found living relationship with Jesus, Marian Adair was almost daily ringing Alicia up to tell her of some new and exciting lesson she was learning in the new life.

The Hon. E. Ross Adair stated in the Congressional Record of January 18, 1960 an extension of the remarks he made in the House of Representatives: "The clue to Alicia Abrahamsen's ministry lies in her statement, ' The deeper spiritual life is an absolute necessity to live the victorious life and have the overflowing life that is a blessing to others. The world is hungry for reality, and we have failed to make Christ real in our lives. We are so apt to become self-righteous or narrow and condemning. Christ wants us to be in love with Him, so that everyone who comes into our presence might sense the loveliness of Christ.' Alicia Abrahamsen does more than say it. She lives it. And therein lies the success of her witness in Washington." Both Congressman Adair and his wife also "live it." They have made "Christ their Campaign Manager," and when people ask them how they can help, they say "Pray." His majority in the election went up from hundreds to several thousand and they now "can't think why it took them ten years to find this secret out."

The grandchildren, too, know they have a playmate in Grandpa Abram. Recently little Kevin Abram, son of his young-

est boy, faithful standby at the home base, now living in Harris-
burg, was left for a few days in charge of the grandparents at
Fellowship House. Abram's daughter-in-law recounts upon
their return they were rather disappointed not to receive from
him a warmer welcome. As they stood in the hall little Kevin
ran to the foot of the stairs and looked up. "Grandpa!" he said,
with his face all aglow. Abram was coming down the stairs.

Abram had the gift of creating confidence in his children,
which made them want to do what was right, simply because
of the faith he had in them. But that faith was not in some in-
nate goodness in them—he knew the truth better than that—but
because he believed they belonged to God. An illustration of
that was a letter his son Milton wrote him from Princeton
Seminary. Milton and his wife Bonnie are now Presbyterian
missionaries in the Philippines and also active in I.C.L.: "Dear
Dad, Thought about you today when I sat eating a very
delicious chicken dinner, I thought about the sacrifices you are
making to perform your mission over there. We follow your
activities with great interest and prayer. Your letter written
to me while on board ship made me very proud to be your son.
I feel very unworthy of your pride in me. I do pray that the
Lord will use me in the vineyard. . . ."

On that European visit, Abram had written to Mattie:

On Boardship

7-2-47

The ship is just pulling out and I am alone in my cabin.
After you left, I had to go and be with God in prayer. It
was easy to weep then—and I felt lonely. What a treasure
you are! Now here alone with God for five days I will be
much in prayer for you all and the work. It must be deeply
spiritual. God's Word must have the prominent place.
Jesus Christ must have the pre-eminence. Oh, how I long
to glorify His name—honor Him who died for me. As I
proceed on this mission, I recognize my utter dependence
on *Him*. There is a sense of comfort and deep joy in the
fact that *He* is with me. He will *never* fail me or leave me
alone.

We have so much to live for, fight for and, if need be,
to die for. Building and maintaining creative fellowship

on a world scale—through it all win people for Christ. Here is constant joyous teamwork till the end of the journey. We will not think of ourselves. It is so easy to coddle, pamper or excuse self. But as we do—we begin to die. It is constantly to rise to difficulties, scale new heights and go on with Jesus.

Zurich

8-25-47

This is our wedding day. My love and gratitude goes out to you. What a school these 37 years have been. How good and patient you have been! What a joy in service, home, children and fellowship! Praise God for it all. Real satisfaction comes through service and self-giving to God and men. In a common cause of Christ and the Kingdom we have given our all. He in turn has given us His all including His glory with the Father. "For the joy that was set before Him—He endured the cross." We too have endured at times the cross in a minor way, but oh, the joys and the blessings! I wouldn't change with the richest.

18 | WHAT HAPPENS IN THE GROUPS

By means of a monthly letter which was first merely headed, "Breakfast Groups" (of which there are now two hundred in this country alone), and later enlarged as a bulletin under the title "Christian Leadership," Abram circulates a Bible discussion outline and challenge for each week of the month. Breakfast Groups use them as the basis of their weekly fellowship.

Not all the groups are by any means as strong as they should be. This is particularly so where there is not a leader of spiritual understanding. The purpose of the groups is to welcome men who often have no clear Christian commitment; and if there is not at least one among them able to present the Christian faith in living and intelligible terms, there may be groups that have as yet no firm foundations in the faith. But at least all have the message plainly enough in print in the weekly outline.

The aim is that Bible reading should be foremost in every group, otherwise talk can go all over the place. Fireside groups are also emphasized. They are superior to Breakfast Groups in the respect that those who attend them do not have to hurry away, and problems can be more thoroughly dealt with.

In one month alone, news from the different groups included the witness of these men, named only by their initial:

Mr. D. went to his office from a breakfast meeting some time ago, reflecting on the Scripture discussion and the testimonies of the hour. He recognized that it was not so much a matter of demanding from others, as of demonstrating in his own life. He was aware of things that needed to be adjusted with himself, some things eliminated and a revised order of living. This was not easy, but he knew it was right and it was his duty towards himself, his family, his business, his city and his God. He went on his knees to ask God for forgiveness for past failures and to yield himself in utter commitment, to be God's man and to carry out His will. In doing this, new light and power came.

In this new-found release, it became natural for him to translate ideas into action. He met with one of his associates with whom there had been a misunderstanding, and that was cleared up. He met with his staff, with whom there now developed a frank and genuine teamwork to do business under God's direction. A regular meeting was inaugurated with both business and department heads, where prayer was a regular feature.

"I never saw this before," said Mr. B., "but now I realize that if men, regardless of background and religious affiliation, will only begin to meet together in honest and frank fellowship, to learn God's will and His plan for life, the answer will come and the solution will be found. Power and inspiration will come to each man's life. The Bible has it. The Holy Spirit gives it. Jesus Christ is the hope of every man."

He invited at least one new man each week to the breakfast club. He usually paid for his breakfast the first time, and then kept telephoning or bringing him to the meeting for two or three times, till the man became sufficiently inoculated to continue under his own steam. He then proceeded to inaugurate other groups, recognizing that a group is usually more effective when it is limited to 12 to 20 in regular attendance.

"The drive for more aggressive action," said Mr. R., "came after a period of prayer. When I unloaded on God, God began to unload on me. My interest was centered on the colored people, their rights and their place. I interested a group of their leaders in beginning to meet as a breakfast group. I found these men to be drunk with the sense of their rights, but after a period together with the Bible and with Christ, they, like the rest of us, became imbued with a sense of duty and responsibility."

A prominent Republican at a recent House of Representatives breakfast meeting, stated, "We Republicans pray God to give us more Democrats like Percy Priest of Tennessee. His life and his spirit, as well as his words in Congress, are a living testimony to the reality of the Christian faith and the Christian religion."

From an I.C.L. group in England that same month came the following: "After a depression that left me mentally and physically exhausted, I was sitting alone one evening with my miserable thoughts when a complete stranger came and sat near me. My condition must have shown on my face, for he started talking about Christ and 'the life.' I was invited to an I.C.L. meeting and, as I was in a state to 'try anything,' I went along.

"I was agreeably surprised at the warmth of welcome accorded me and immediately life seemed better. I continued my attendance at the meetings regularly and obtained much mental and spiritual benefit, but still had not given myself to Christ and asked Him to come into my life. At a later meeting the speaker was Stanley Browne, the most remarkable man I have ever met. He spoke of his life story and conversion. I came to know this man intimately. He gave much of his time, daily encouraging me to release my worries to Christ and teaching me how to live again, for I had definitely been in a living death. At the end of a week I found that I could pray aloud with him to God and I asked Christ to come into my life. He did and life became brighter and full. I realized my past selfishness and started to put things right, trying to make amends for my faults. To me the results were astounding; difficulties disappeared and relationships improved immediately. I now had practical proof of the power of Christ within me. My whole outlook changed. I have yet far to go and much to put right to make up for my years of self, but now I *know* Christ is with me, leading the way."

Vereide had issued a challenge earlier that year, 1949, in one of his Breakfast Group leaflets: "Christianity in Action is not limited to eight hours a day, and five and a half working days a week—there is no vacation. 'My Father worketh until now and I work.' Everywhere and all the time you and I are the representatives of Jesus Christ. The cab driver may be a prospect for the Kingdom, so I seek the opportunity to get into a conversation with him, give him encouragement, and if the Spirit so leads, to 'close the deal' and help him to a definite decision and pray with him before I leave. The boy or the girl in the elevator, the delivery man, the mailman, the attendant in the gas station, the maid at the hotel, but first of all my associates in business and my own family. I 'begin at Jerusalem.' While all of us are, therefore, the representatives of Christ, we must do like the early disciples did. Everywhere they went they spread the good news and were the contagious forces drawing all men unto Him. We seek to concentrate on leadership and ask:

1. How may the political leadership of city, state and nation, be won for Christ?
2. How may we win the business leadership of this community to Christ?
3. What may be done to win industry for Christ?
4. How may we win our educational leaders for Christ?

Week by week let us encourage and help each other; week by week let us produce results, and win men for Christ, His Church and His Kingdom."

In a personal visit in 1951 to a group started in 1935, where a hundred men gathered to welcome him, he gave the encouraging report: "One man told about his life in his office with his associates and employees. There was understanding and teamwork. Problems were ironed out with honesty and frankness. God was a partner. A lawyer related how he had to decline to represent a concern that offered him very large annual remuneration, because he could not as an honest and honorable Christian represent that kind of business. A leader of labor reported on how the new approach as a Christian was working out in his field. The mayor of a city and other city officers, the governor of a state and men in various industrial capacities, had a witness on the effectiveness of the way of Christ as the only way, for it is the way that is written into the very constitution of things, from the human body to every phase of human relationship. There had been failures, but the failures had been only to the degree that this or that one had failed to put first things first and maintain a union with the Source, Jesus."

The 20th anniversary of the Breakfast Groups in Seattle was made a great occasion for Vereide. Many old friends gathered, and the Seattle Pacific College conferred on him the honorary degree of L.L.D. An original and effective use was made of the occasion by some who were crossing from the east coast. Two teams of witness were flown in two private planes by their owners, one from the South and one from the East. One plane belonged to Ford Mason, president of the Ford Mason Gum Machine Co. of Akron, New York, who runs his firm for God and is a wholehearted supporter of I.C.L. He flew his plane from Buffalo to the capital cities of a number of the northwestern states. The senators representing each state over which they were flying wrote their state governors, telling them of what Mr. Vereide meant to them in Congress, and suggesting that they give a welcome to the party flying to his anniversary. The governors responded with generous hospitality, arranging luncheons and dinners in their capitals, where the team had the opportunity of witnessing to the state officials, sometimes numbering one hundred. The plane made landings at Pierre, South Dakota; Cheyenne, Wyoming; Helena, Montana; Boise, Idaho; Salem, Oregon; and the party finally received a tremendous welcome from Governor Langlie in Olympia, Washington. The governor had been one of the first in whose heart the Spirit of God had done a work in those early Seattle meetings. Most of the guests at the various receptions had not heard about I.C.L. before. The other plane flew up from Alabama to Seattle, stopping at the three state capitals of Alabama, Arkansas, and Colorado.

19 | THE PRESIDENTIAL PRAYER BREAKFASTS

When the head of a great nation gives some voluntary evidence that his is a leadership led by God, not by attending some religious service which is part of his normal duty, but by some spontaneous witness to his faith, the impression is bound to be great and the influence far-reaching: and we may also be sure that the old word still stands true through the centuries: "Them that honor Me, I will honor."

When the man who does this is head of the world's greatest nation, the nation which confronts in sharpest opposition the other claimant to world leadership based on a defiant atheism, the witness to his living faith is worldwide, not nationwide.

Dwight D. Eisenhower did this on two notable occasions. The first was the prayer he himself wrote and read without warning to a startled and approving nation at his Inaugural Ceremony. The second was his consent to attend with members of his cabinet, Senate, and Congress, the Dedicatory Prayer Breakfast of the annual conference of I.C.L. This put prayer, because of the President's message that morning, on the front page of all the newspapers. Prayer made headlines. It also had the effect, though not indeed planned for that purpose, of bringing the existence of the I.C.L. and the chain of Breakfast Groups across the country to the attention of the nation. God does that kind of thing, when men walk with Him in sincerity and obedience, as Abram Vereide and his team were doing, not for personal aggrandizement nor for the propagation of a movement, but with the single aim of pointing to the King and the Kingdom. The sudden moment comes when, without premeditation, God makes it known openly that His seal is on His servants and that He has raised up another agency of worldwide witness.

It was not to I.C.L., however, that the President was giving honor by his attendance and message, but to God, and expressing by this means the need of His guidance in his great responsibility.

The first Presidential Prayer Breakfast at the Mayflower Hotel in Washington, February 5, 1953. President Eisenhower with Abraham Vereide and the Hon. Katharine St. George M.C., on his right, and Senator Carlson, President of I.C.L. International, and Conrad Hilton, the host of the Breakfast, on his left.

The 1953 Breakfast was held at the Mayflower Hotel in Washington, D.C. The invitation necessarily had to be limited to delegates and some guests. It was an informal occasion much like ordinary breakfast meetings, with the exception that participation in the program was limited to the few at the head table. These were the President of the United States, who was the principal speaker, Senator Frank Carlson, chairman of the breakfast and president of the International Council of Christian Leadership, Conrad Hilton, the host, the Hon. Katharine St. George, member of Congress for New York State, who gave the opening prayer and Scripture. The dedicatory prayer presenting the new cabinet and appointed officials to God for His guidance and blessing was given by Abram Vereide.

There was no publicity, although many newspaper notices appeared, for such an unusual occasion could not but attract attention. Over five hundred were present, including Vice President Nixon, the Cabinet and White House officials, and members of the Supreme Court, the Senate and House of Representatives. All except the speakers had to find their own places as best they could, and be seated with anyone regardless of rank, in "a fellowship of the concerned whose hope is in God." A White House stenographer was present and took down the proceedings verbatim. They were inserted in the Congressional Record for Tuesday, February 10, 1953, by Senator Carlson.

As Abram said afterwards, "Here were free citizens in a free country gathering together regardless of party and creed, zealous for the truth, and for right relationships both with God and man. These are men who ask not so much who is right as what is right; men who recognize that persons without principles are dangerous, and that principles without persons are useless; but that persons plus principles are the great assets everywhere."

In the account written by Dr. Frederick Brown Harris, the Chaplain of the Senate, and published in the *Washington Star*, he said: "There can be no doubt about it, even in Government-centered Washington there is a new surge of reality, so far as vital religion is concerned. The Return-to-God Movement is more than a slogan. Prayer is actually being practiced, not just as a means of getting something from God but as an open channel to get to God and to find and be found by God himself the only adequate answer to human need. There is the sound of a going in the tops of the mulberry trees, not only along the Potomac but across this wide land. There are signs that once again, as in the former days of the Nation's true glory, America is bending its knees. There are increasing numbers of those in high places of governance and industry whose solemn and serious attitude is: 'I want to be a Christian, in my heart.'

"It is not the repetition of a formal creed; it is a repudiation of practical atheism, of the deadly materialism which has degraded and cursed American life and which will damn it if not stopped.

"The dramatic action on inaugural day, of the man who had been President only a few moments, in asking the country and the world to join him in prayer, exactly fits into the mood now so exhilaratingly apparent. When the simple petitions of the new Chief Executive, pleading for help to the Father God, fell on the ears of listening hosts expectantly lining the Avenue for the parade, one who was half a mile from the Capitol said that, as over the amplifier the praying voice resounded, there was an electric something that seemed to summon the waiting multitudes to their knees. And across the Nation that mystic thrill was registered. That supplication turned the inaugural platform into a high and holy altar. It came from a deeply held conviction regarding the inevitable finality of spiritual verities.

"This new under-God consciousness, which is gripping our leaders, is, of course, no partisan affair. Party shibboleths have absolutely nothing to do with it. It is infinitely bigger than that. For a long while under the white dome members of the Senate and the House, without thought of political affiliation, have met weekly for a fellowship of prayer.

"There occurred in the Capital City on February the 5th one of the most amazing prayer meetings ever held since Washington agonized on the frozen ground of Valley Forge. Originally there was visualized but a small group at this morning altar of prayer. But the idea grew, and so many begged to come that finally, about 400 sat down to breakfast in the Mayflower Hotel ballroom, with Senator Frank Carlson of Kansas as the leader of this national service of prayer.

"It was shortly after 8 a.m. that a figure emerged through

the iron gates of the White House grounds. It was Dwight
Eisenhower on his way to the prayer meeting. Awaiting, when
he arrived, was the Chief Justice of the United States and
associate justices of the Supreme Court, members of the cabinet, many Senators and Representatives and leaders in various
professions and in industry. There were no pictures taken. And
there was no applause. Even when the President stood to
speak, that company simply arose in silence. It was the atmosphere of a sanctuary, and the usual trappings of public affairs
would have seemed sacrilege.

"The President in an unpremeditated address poured out
his soul regarding the primacy of 'deeply felt religion' as this
crisis is faced. 'Prayer,' he declared, 'is simply a necessity.' It
was the desire of the President that one of the prayers in this
high hour might be for the leaders of the new administration.
He sat with head reverently bowed while the following petition
was lifted:

" 'God, our Father, we thank Thee for the man who in Thy
providence has become our Chief Executive, to administer the
affairs of this Nation, and for the men selected by him for their
various responsibilities. We now present these men to Thee
and beseech Thee to grant unto them Thy grace and guidance,
wisdom, insight and understanding. Save them from self-
deception, conceit, and the folly of independence of Thee, O
God,' that we may indeed have a leadership led by Thee.'

"High above that great praying Breakfast Group was a striking colored picture of Uncle Sam on his knees, with clasped
hands and upturned face. And beside that kneeling form was
engraved a prayer shot through with the grace of national
penitence. That poster portrays America on its knees—not
beaten there by the hammer and sickle, but freely, intelli-
gently, responsibly, fearing nothing or no one except God. And
here, in part, are the searching sentences of that confession to
the Eternal:

" 'Our Father, we pray that you will save us from ourselves.
We have turned from you to go our selfish way. We have broken
your commandments and denied your truth. We have left
your altars to serve the false gods of money and pleasure and
power. Now, darkness gathers round us and we are confused in
all our councils. Losing faith in You we lose faith in ourselves.

Inspire us with wisdom, all of us, of every color, race and creed, to use our wealth and our strength to help our brother, instead of destroying him. Fill us with new faith, new strength and new courage, that we may win the battle for peace. Be swift to save us, dear God, before the darkness falls.' "

Billy Graham was present at this breakfast, and he added this comment: "If our people could have felt what I have felt and seen what I have seen here this day, a great surge of new hope would well up in their hearts and in their souls concerning the future of our way of life. On the way out this morning from the Breakfast the Chief Justice of the Supreme Court, Judge Vinson, made this comment to me: 'I have never felt or seen anything like this meeting in all my years here in Washington.' "

The Presidential Breakfast of 1956 was notable for the presentation made to the President by Conrad Hilton of a silver plaque with the prayer which he had written and offered at his inauguration inscribed on it. The President was not announced to speak at the breakfast, but he did so extemporaneously. "Mr. Chairman, Mr. Hilton, and my friends," he said, "this is a touching thing which Mr. Hilton has done in presenting to me this plaque and the desk and chair from which I wrote the little prayer that I used at the inauguration some three years ago. That incident brought to me a great message. It seemed to me a perfectly natural thing to do. I was seeking some way to impress upon the audience at that moment that all of us realized a new chief executive would be inaugurated over a nation that was founded on a religious faith. Our founding documents so state in explaining our Government and what we intended to do.

"In the Declaration of Independence are found references to the Creator which gave us certain rights in our Government, and it was set up to sustain them. That seemed to me a perfectly natural thing to do as a method of showing that I also believed. It was with some astonishment that I began to see this response. Literally thousands of messages came in, some of them from people who did not particularly think I was the man to occupy the place. They still applauded that act. Here is the lesson as I see it. I know very few men, very few people, who tell me they are atheists or agnostics. But we find among the laity a curious diffidence in merely stating the

Abraham Vereide with President Eisenhower.

Dr. Vereide with four men who participated in the 1954 Prayer Breakfast. (l. to r.) Secretary of the Army, Wilbur M. Brucker; Senator Frank Carlson; Vice President Richard Nixon; Judge Boyd Leedom, Chairman of the Labor Relations Board and President of International Christian Leadership.

Photo by Seth Muse

fact that they believe there is a God and that He is more powerful than they and they depend upon Him. That is what the prayer was for. It was because a layman did do so, and of course in such a position, that this response came in. I think that prayer is somewhat related to these Prayer Breakfasts. We can pray in our quarters, but we can also come to gatherings occasionally—and I understand this whole meeting is a week long —announcing to the world that we come as laymen and meet, making the same acknowledgment that was made in that prayer and doing exactly the same thing. We are telling people that this nation is still a nation under God. This is terrifically important today. . . .

"I had no intention of making a speech. As a matter of fact, I was promised I didn't have to, and I don't know how I got started."

In the breakfast of the next year, 1957, with the President present, Chief Justice Earl Warren gave the leading address, with the president of I.C.L. Senator Frank Carlson, in the chair. In the course of Senator Carlson's remarks, he gave some history of the birth and growth of I.C.L., describing it as living Christianity versus militant materialism.

"The Breakfast Groups," he said, "are calling thinking men and women in every area to honesty, with repentance toward God and faith in the Lord Jesus Christ. The Bible has become a living book, the one central source for inspiration, comfort, and instruction in righteousness; prayer, a practical reality, and Jesus Christ, the eternal contemporary as Saviour and Lord. The irrefutable evidence of the reality of the Christian faith is the Christian man or woman who embodies the mind, the Spirit of Christ. We do not represent a political party or denomination, but we are representatives of the people as a whole who have found a common denominator for effective teamwork and service in daily life. It is not only the fellowship of the concerned, but it is a fellowship of believers whose faith prompts action and sacrificial living.

"We are again rediscovering that God who was in Christ, reconciling the world unto Himself, has come to live in us by His Spirit. We are convinced that the answer to all our problems finds a basic solution through a spiritual rebirth and the revival of genuine religion. This morning we are here to renew our faith and our commitment to God."

20 | MINISTERING TO ROYALTY

Vereide's journals are crammed with the names of men. There is no doubt where his heart and vision lie. It is not in an organization, not in a creed, but in *people*, in men. As he once exclaimed on seeing a new bird, "What a variety in God's creation! What fun He must have in creation! We are instruments for Him to create new things too—new men and women through whom come new expressions of His glory."

Read through the pages of his journals for the 17 years since they came to Washington, and more often than not it is just lists of names, prayed for, called on, consulted with, hundreds of them, some world famous names in many countries, others in the van of Christian evangelism.

Constant traveling, all over this country and many times to Europe, despite the coronary occlusion he suffered in 1953 and an uncertain heart condition ever since with fatigue and danger signals when overstrained; addresses to many kinds of audiences, parliamentary meetings in England, Germany, Holland, Norway and other countries; speaking in churches and cathedrals, at breakfast groups and conferences; the person to person contacts which are his special metier; the ever-rolling stream of correspondence; and I.C.L. and Fellowship House constant activities—these have filled the days and years to the brim. But putting warm flesh on the skeleton entries of the journals, every now and then there come paragraphs, even half pages, of the love he has for his Lord. That is his secret. The source of his freshness of spirit is the early hour spent daily with God and the messages and Scriptures often recorded.

On his 66th birthday in 1952, he wrote in his journal: "66 years old. How strange. I don't feel like it. I am yet young and just beginning to live. True, my body is not what it used to be, but I am more alive than ever. My interests are greater, my horizons are larger and my concern is more inclusive. I am identified with all the affairs of the Kingdom as the King's ambassador. Oh how wonderful to be alive—to think, to feel, to see, to hear, to understand, to know, to mingle with men and to be in love with all, because God's love is in me. He loves men through me. He floods me with His life, light and love. Glory, glory, Hallelujah!"

In 1953: "I am the Lord's. I am here to please Him and glorify His name in a life of holiness and self-effacing service. Lord, use me this day, live in me and through me—Amen."

On his seventieth birthday in 1956: "Lord Jesus, thank you. I begin again at 70—by thy grace. No desire but to please Thee, and love Thee only and all people in Thee. 'The world passeth away and the lust thereof, but he that doeth the will of God abideth forever.' Live in His will—*be* His will."

And in the same year: "O God, how great and wonderful Thou art! I love and adore Thee. By Thee, through, for and to Thee are all things. Here am I also a part of Thy great purpose. Living with a sense of responsibility. *I am* a new creation—a new species in Christ—for an eternal destiny. Instead of looking at myself, I look at Him, and as I do, I am being changed. In this I glory and my whole being is filled with praise."

In another entry: "What an inspiring and wonderful privilege to be part of a global fellowship that transcends race, creed, language, and nationality, each seeking the other's good, all conscious of a Person and an eternal purpose, a power beyond that of atomic energy, a warmth of congeniality because of the indwelling Spirit of infinite love. This is the Church ecumenical, the Church on the march in many different branches, organizations, and agencies. Here are Christian laymen refusing to quibble about the less essentials, uniting to serve, determined to understand, committed to truth and love."

Abram's closest links in Europe have been with the Dutch Royal Family. Her Royal Highness, Princess Wilhelmina, the heroic former Queen of The Netherlands, had been the focal point of the Nation's resistance to German enslavement in World War II, when she lived in exile in England. On her return she had passed the burdens of the crown to her daughter Juliana. Some who heard Abraham Vereide speak in Holland in the summer of 1950 on Christian Leadership told Princess Wilhelmina about him and he was summoned to Het Loo

Palace. Before leaving, Her Royal Highness sent him to see her daughter, the Queen. From these times of ever-deepening fellowship, which included Prince Bernhard, came the planning of the first Noordwijk conference in May 1952 and Her Royal Highness' acceptance of the honorary presidency of I.C.L.

On his first visit, Abram began talking to Her Royal Highness about world events; but she said, "Mr. Vereide, there are many who can talk to me about these matters. Will you talk to me about Jesus?" There have been many visits since, gathering with the Royal Family in prayer, Bible study, and conference.

In his considerable correspondence with her he wrote at various times:

Washington, January 28, 1955

Ma'am:

The great gathering at the Presidential Breakfast was greatly inspired by your cable message which was read. . . . Your inspiring letter and Christmas greetings brought me much joy. I am deeply grateful. It gladdened me also to learn about the well-being of your daughter and family. It is a happy privilege to bring you all to God in prayer each day with much thanksgiving . . .

I was reading this morning about Mary—how "That Holy Thing which shall be born of thee shall be called the Son of God." It was something from the beyond which became the within and produced the new man—the God-Man. Is it not when that something from beyond, the Holy Spirit, comes within and we are born into the full consciousness of God as a Father that we can begin to give adequate expression through our purified and God-controlled faculties to God's life and His principles in our actions and relationships?

I find that *the human spirit fails unless the Holy Spirit fills*. I also find the need of the daily and continual renewal, and to do what Jesus told us, saying, "If ye abide in me and my words abide in you, you shall . . ." The great bulk of Christendom remains on the periphery in a rather superficial attachment to the Church, yet I am so thankful for the increasing number of men in all walks of life who are going deeper and, as a result, are getting farther. In the rush of modern life, it is difficult to be disciplined to the quiet hour, and to be still and know that He is God. But herein lies the secret. . . .

I believe God will give us a great year with new advances on every front, for His is "the Kingdom, the power, and the glory."

Please give my hearty regards to Her Majesty.

Joyfully and thankfully yours,
Abraham Vereide

March 16, 1955

Ma'am:

Everywhere there is evidence of the spring of the Spirit, the quickening from on high. Thank God for the privilege we have on being part of this great global outreach to discover, promote and cultivate a leadership led by God.

How gracious you are in extending to me the invitation to be your guest. I would appreciate the privilege of unhurried time to visit together about the things of God and His Word. The disciples on the Emmaus road relate how their hearts burned within them, as Jesus came and walked with them and opened the Scriptures. May this be our experience too. . . .

April 2, 1958

Ma'am:

On Sunday I stayed in my room all day to be utterly secluded with the Lord and His Word. It was a wonderful day. Jesus took with Him Peter, James and John and went apart to meditate and pray. They saw Moses and Elijah. They heard a voice through the cloud, and then they saw no man save Jesus. He is the Ultimate Reality. How wonderful to be in union with Him as a branch of the Vine! What a privilege to be utterly yielded to Him and to let Him live in us through faith and obedience. I am so glad that these experiences are universal and timeless. The experiences of His life in us in the realm of the mundane, in the simple, ordinary things of life. We are aware of His majestic strides through history and His wonderful guiding principles and power in world affairs, toward the one great culmination of all things, but also of His comforting Presence which is constant.

I rejoice in His sustaining grace and power in your life, Your Royal Highness. What an inspiration and power of strength you are! I eagerly look forward to the fellowship with you in September. May there be a time before the Conference to muse, meditate, pray and counsel together, thinking through the Conference with an eye on the personalities that will be there, and objectives before us? I plan to fly direct from here to Holland some time in advance of the Conference, September 8 to 14.

With my deepest respect and affectionate greetings, I beg Your Royal Highness, to remain,

Respectfully yours,
Abraham Vereide

Noordwijk is a beautiful Dutch seaside resort. At the first Conference, in 1952, there was a gathering of 250 people from positions of major responsibility in twelve different countries, including three United States Senators, Flanders, Wiley and Carlson. Princess Wilhelmina was in attendance the five days, and gave the opening and closing messages. Her Majesty Queen Juliana was in attendance three days and addressed the conference.

Before arrival, Abram had written to his wife:

5-20-52

In two hours and twenty minutes we land in Paris. Here too rages the battle for men's minds. The materialistic concept of life creates havoc everywhere. The dance around the golden calf—the work of our own hands, the glory of the seen and the allurement of the sensual have intoxicated men living in the realm of sense knowledge only. "The natural man cannot comprehend the things of God—the things of the Spirit," said Paul. Man must be born from above—of the Spirit, to become balanced, understanding and adequate.

Such men in each country need to know each other—on the same level—in order to produce global team work. Those who have found the Light, who know the Way, must assist those who search and want to find, who desire to know, and then under the guidance of God work together where they are and in international affairs. So we meet as International Christian Leadership for the annual meeting of the Council at The Hague —May 22–25. Senator Flanders is the chairman. Her Royal

Dr. Vereide, H.R.H. Princess Wilhelmina, and Mr. John Henderson M.P. at Noordwijk, The Netherlands, 1956.

Her Majesty Queen Juliana of the Netherlands, Senator Ralph Flanders, H.R.H. Princess Wilhelmina (with Abraham Vereide seated behind) at the first I.C.L. Conference in Noordwijk, Holland, 1952   Photos by B. Ietswaart

Highness Princess Wilhelmina is the honorary chairman. These two will alternate presiding. Her Majesty Queen Juliana will address the Conference Friday. General Gruenther on Saturday. Senators Wiley and Carlson and Congressman Armstrong Saturday and Sunday. Men with a message from many countries will be there. God will be there.

This being the first major international conference, Vereide outlined the aims of I.C.L.: "Here in staid Europe, rooted in convention, anchored to tradition, sobered by history and fearful of tomorrow, political, industrial and military leaders are casting about for solutions in their efforts to build a sound economy, a peaceful society and a needed strength.

"We have come for the moral and spiritual undergirding in these efforts. We are keenly conscious of three distinct issues:

"First, the issue between two conflicting ideas about the form of human society: the totalitarian idea now identified with the Russian form of Communism, and the idea of free democracy. We recognize that the latter means the preservation of the essential liberties of the individual, and that we cannot fight the forces of totalitarianism effectively merely by arming ourselves, or destroy it by a contrary doctrine. Words will not suffice, nor will weapons of war bring salvation. The only way to defeat the wrong form of Communism is to make a success of our own form of society. Since ours is now essentially an industrial society, the first condition of success is to insure, not only that our industry is organized to fulfill the necessary social purposes, but also and still more important, that industrial employment can provide a foundation for worthy human lives.

"Second, beneath this issue lies another, and of more profound significance: the issue between those on the one hand who hold that might is right, that man is master of his life and is his own lawmaker, and on the other hand those who believe that there is a higher law based on absolute standards of right and wrong, which man can never in any circumstance justifiably disregard.

"Third, underlying this is a third issue: the issue between those who do not look beyond this worldly life, and those to whom religious faith must be the guide for all their thoughts and actions. The observance of absolute laws of right and wrong is impossible by ordinary human beings except on the foundation of religious faith, which for us, representatives of Christendom as a whole, means the Christian faith. This is the greatest issue of all, the one on which all others depend.

"The fundamental need before us is, therefore, the revival of Christian faith as a living force in all human activities. The emphasis must be on the ethical principles of religion applied in daily life and to every issue, born from a consciousness of God and the individual experience of the transforming power of Jesus Christ as Saviour from sin and the Lord of life. Herein lies the answer to men who are groping for something to give meaning to their lives."

Princess Wilhelmina opened the conference by saying, "In the name of Christ, as President of the 1952 Conference of the International Council for Christian Leadership, I call this Conference into session.

"Friends and members of the International Council for Christian Leadership from our two continents, it is a source of joy to me to welcome you here today in our country at Noordwijk on Sea. . . .

"It is almost above our power of conception to understand that the supreme love of our Redeemer descends and penetrates at this very moment in all man's activities and expressions of life with the purpose of raising them to a degree where man will be able to live according to His Word. . . .

"Before, however, attempting to seek for a solution in the entanglements of today, we should first of all give our full attention to the spiritual regeneration of humanity.

"Mankind is yearning to experience a Christianity made real. . . ."

The Princess followed it by a broadcast message after the conference in which she declared: "Young men and young women! Remember that Christ Himself tells us to come to Him, to listen to Him and to act, like the man who built a house and digged deep until he struck on the Rock and thereupon he laid the foundation, and the coming floods could not shake it.

"Remove all that Christ and your conscience disqualifies until you strike on the Rock, which is Christ Himself. Then lay the foundation He teaches you. The only one on which our reborn Europe can arise unshakable against all floods."

The 1952 conference was historic because it was the break-

Mr. Vereide with Gustav-Adolf Gedat, Md.B., founder of I.C.L. in Germany.

The historic Ridderzaal Meeting when Germans and Dutch found fellowship in Christ in 1952. Dr. Ehlers, President of the Bundestag speaking; Vereide facing speaker on the left.

Photo by B. Ietswaart

down of the barriers between Germany and Holland and the other European countries. A delegation of forty Germans, at the invitation of I.C.L. President Gustav Gedat Md. B., had arrived for the first time since the War. The president of the German Bundestag was Dr. Ehlers, the chief delegate to the conference from Bonn. He spoke at the concluding session in the Ridderzaal at The Hague, the historic national center for the opening of Parliament, where the Queen's throne stands from which she reads her message to the Parliament. It was also from here the infamous Nazi general condemned many a Dutchman to the firing squad. So it was daring to have a German appear in such a sacred place in Holland, where animosity and bitterness had prevailed since the War and where the German language was not heard.

Margot Amies, one of the I.C.L. staff, described the scene: "The Ridderzaal is the old Knight's Hall where the Queen addresses the two Houses of Parliament. It is simply beautiful, with a ceiling rather like that of Westminster Hall in London. Beautiful rich tapestries are hung all round the walls and thick rugs on the floor. There is a big dais in the center, and under a canopy are the two thrones—one much bigger than the other. Shields and coats of arms are hung all round the walls too—stained glass windows, and from the ceiling hang the most exquisite lights I have ever seen. They are like twinkling diamonds arranged in many large circles. A great Dutch choir of one hundred male voices sang superbly. I had no idea it would be anything so wonderful. It was completely out of this world—a great spiritual blessing for all, and they received tremendous applause. I have never heard anything like it in my life before."

"Then followed several addresses; but when Dr. Ehlers rose to speak in German, the atmosphere was electric with tension. As he went on, he told how he too had suffered under Hitler, and he asked the Dutch people to forgive the German nation for the great suffering they had brought upon them. It was only in Christ that true understanding between the peoples of Europe could come again. He then summoned all in repentance and renewed faith to begin to rebuild the nations on a Christian foundation. As he sat down, there was a great silence and a sudden sense of relief. The tension was broken. Abraham Vereide's countenance radiated the spiritual victory that had been won in that memorable hour, as the great choir sang its closing number. From that came the breaking down of barriers and the re-establishment of better relations.

At the Ladies' Breakfast Group at Noordwijk the following Sunday morning, after the church services and Holy Communion, Countess de Gontaut Biron, a leader of the French underground who was imprisioned one year at Ravensbruck, stood up to say she had that morning forgiven her former enemies, whereupon Margrit Gaertener of I.C.L. Berlin, rose to ask forgiveness for her countrymen with tears streaming down her face. The ice was permanently broken at that moment between the Dutch, French, and Germans. In fact, since then they have visited one another in group meetings and retreats in their respective countries, and have exchanged visits of mutual helpfulness. Two women brought this meeting about— Ella Gronroos of Helsinki, leader of the powerful Women's Prayer Group in Finland during the war, and Josie Lashar of New York. That evening there followed a most beautiful time of witnessing to victory and release through the Spirit and love of Jesus Christ.

Two years ago Vereide verified from high sources the reality of the outcome of those meetings. Historians noted the change in relations between the countries concerned, but they could record only the outward facts. They do not know the spiritual background, the turning point which the 1952 conference proved to be.

21 | I.C.L. IN MANY LANDS

It was not until Wallace Haines, with his wife, Frances, and their three sons, answered the call of God to make their home in Europe as permanent I.C.L. representatives, that the movement began to take root in various European countries. Wallace joined the I.C.L. in 1951. He had known Mr. Vereide in the early days in Chicago, and he wrote asking if he could be of service to him on his 1951 tour in Germany. It was at the Castle

Mainau Conference on Lake Constance, inaugurated by Gustav Gedat and attended by the Bishop of Worms, Prince Hohenlohe and other prominent Germans, that Wallace Haines caught the vision of I.C.L. as a bridge-building movement to bring reconciliation between the nations in the aftermath of the war. Democracy is concommitant with spiritual revival. In promoting our way of democracy to Europeans, many Americans coming to Europe, including Christian missionaries, did not know how to work in Europe after the war. A dynamic speaker with a God-given message of reconciliation, Wallace made a deep impression at the closing meeting of the Mainau Conference and subsequently on the German groups that he and Gedat visited, because he was understanding of their particular needs; and this was to prove even more true with the work he was to begin the following year in France.

Wallace Haines and his family made Paris their home. God implanted in them a deep and sincere love for the French people who, with all their rich culture and intellectual brilliance, yet for the most part are out of touch with spiritual realities. With a hope and a faith for a spiritual renaissance, they started with the nation's leaders. Senator Edmond Michelet, now Minister of Justice in the de Gaulle government, was one of the first to respond; a warm, vital Christian, interned as leading French prisoner at Dachau, and later Minister of War, he has been an unswerving colleague of Abraham Vereide and Wallace Haines in establishing I.C.L. in France and acting as president there. Also participating have been Senator Brunhes, Marcel and Suzanne Bresard, Colette Weiss and Francois Dausset, to mention only a few. Marjorie Wright, who had been secretary for the New York I.C.L. office and headquarters, moved to France and joined the Haineses in devoted pioneering for Christ, until her marriage to another keen I.C.L. member, Dr. Spencer Miller, former U.S. Assistant Secretary of Labor, and her early death a year later.

As the team developed, meetings were held monthly at the Haines's home or at the apartment of Countess de Gontaut Biron, who became with Wallace the leader of the work in Paris. This enthusiastic, vibrant French woman, of Polish birth, had played bridge with Gestapo officers, while running the gauntlet as a resistance leader for General de Gaulle during the Nazi occupation. Now her energies have been directed to bringing men and women under the influence of Christ through I.C.L. Many French and Americans stationed in France with SHAPE or NATO, including General Clovis Byers, then head of the NATO Defense College, have found their way to these evenings of inspiration and challenge.

Compared to the widespread response in the U.S.A., Wallace has often felt that little was happening in France; but not so, when one remembers the wholly different situation, where the country is so strongly divided between clerical and anticlerical sentiment, thousands are openly agnostic and without a vital faith. There are stirrings of life both inside the Roman Church and outside it, such as the now suppressed workerpriest movement under the late Abbé Godin. On one visit, at dinner, Abram sat next to Mme. Hoppenot, who has 2,500 Catholic women in groups of twelve each and was described to Vereide as "the spiritual dynamo in the R.C. church." Ambassador Dillon acted as interpreter. Her face, Abram said, was radiant and "reflected the inner glory." After some conversation, Mme. Hoppenot asked him, "Are you a Protestant?" "Yes." "Then how came you as a Protestant to an experience of Jesus Christ like that?" "Madame," replied Vereide, "how in the world could you as a Roman Catholic come to an experience of Jesus Christ like that"? Then they both laughed!

Both the Countess and Senator Michelet came to a living experience of God in German concentration camps. Senator Michelet has for years been a friend and supporter of General de Gaulle. Another friend of his, a fellow-Christian, is M. Pflimlin, to whom "he was attached in the love of Christ, but from whom on a political level he was widely separated." While M. Pflimlin was a member of the French Parliament, Senator Michelet had brought him to the Noordwijk Conference.

At the time of the French crisis, M. Pflimlin was Premier of France. "He soon recognized his problems," said Senator Michelet, "and remembered over and above political barriers, the I.C.L." He remained in close touch with the Senator in prayer throughout the crisis. Wallace Haines and Bob Pierce, then visiting Paris, also met the Premier personally for prayer, and Wallace telephoned from Holland to I.C.L. in America on behalf of the Premier, who asked him to convey the message that "this is the battle in France to give birth to a new democracy, and he wants I.C.L. and all of you to pray." God heard and answered in the presidency of General de Gaulle and the start of the Fifth Republic.

On a visit in 1956, Abram had met the deputies and senators of the French Parliament, with Ambassador Dillon of the United States. He then spent twenty-five minutes with President Coty, to whom Senator Michelet had introduced him. The President received him, although he was entertaining President Tito of Yugoslavia as a guest at the Palace. Senator Michelet sent the following report of the interview: "After having cordially welcomed Mr. Abraham Vereide and warmly congratulated him upon the objective and the Christian spirit which emanates from I.C.L., President Rene Coty wished to tell him that he had never spoken once in public, since he assumed the responsibility of President of the Republic, without having underlined to the French people the spiritual requirements imposed on our generation before the triple danger that menaces it: that of communism, materialism, and pragmatism.

"The President equally underscored how edified and struck he had been during his stay in Holland, to note the Christian inspiration of all the words and actions of the Queen of the Low Countries.

"Finally in assuring Mr. Vereide of the sentiments of affection of all the French people for General Eisenhower and for President Eisenhower, President Coty asked his visitor to recognize how much in France the situation has evolved spiritually since the time of his own youth sixty years ago. It suffices to enter any church or temple in Paris on a Sunday to perceive that they are always full of men and women. It is sufficient to note the percentage that has risen in theatrical plays and cinemas in Paris consecrated to subjects strictly religious."

To his wife Abram wrote:

Just returned from a most delightful and significant visit with President Coty. He is deeply spiritual, understanding, and a true Christian statesman. Senators Michelet and Brunhes, and Wallace, were along. The old magnificent palace of his residence is far beyond any we have in the U.S.A. The presence of Tito—whom I saw this

149

morning—is creating much of the spectacular. But this meeting with the President was wonderful. He entered into the picture so fully, expressed himself freely, and counselled with us. He sent his greetings to "Ike" and to Queen Juliana and signed our book. The text for Sunday morning (at the American Cathedral) came during the night: "But we see Jesus," Heb. 2:8-9. God's order and man's hope. A personal encounter with Jesus is the one thing that matters.

During that same visit, Vereide spent forty-five minutes with Gen. Norstad, Commander-in-Chief of SHAPE, also with Gen. Gruenther, who had already attended one of the I.C.L. conferences and given an address at it. Mr. Douglas Dillon, the American Ambassador (now Secretary of the U.S. Treasury), told Abram that he had met President Coty at a public function at the Paris Fair on the afternoon of Abram's visit to the President. He had said to Mr. Dillon, "Today I was to have no appointments, but I met one of the finest Americans I have ever met," and he called him "a prophet."

During this mission to Europe, and also on several others, young Dr. Philippe Zuger from Switzerland was of inestimable assistance to Abram.

When Abram first sent Wallace Haines to Europe, he emphasized the fact that, as each national branch of I.C.L. was formed, it must become autonomous and find its own national method of working. The mentality of peoples differ, but it is the same Jesus Christ for all. Nowhere has a national group taken a more distinctive line than in France, as one would expect with such a highly individualistic people.

After the 1958 World Conference, the French felt the time had come for European I.C.L. carefully to prepare a conference of a special type. Minister Michelet invited fifteen leading French journalists to meet at his Palace of Justice to prepare a conference on truth and honesty in propaganda in the press, radio, television, cinema and theater. These experts met several times. At Easter 1959, sixty journalists from five European countries met at Strasbourg together with a hundred other selected members of European I.C.L. Representatives attended from the Assembly of Europe. The dishonesty prevalent in all means of public communication was faced realistically. The

Abraham Vereide's visit to Paris. (l. to r.) Wallace Haines,
European representative of I.C.L.; A.V.; General Gruenther,
NATO Commander-in-Chief; French Minister of Justice
Edmond Michelet.

Official Shape Photo by SP3 W. Kuehlen
& PFC P. Palmquist (US Army).

Meeting on Europe and N. Africa, Mayflower Conference
1957-Abraham Vereide; Countess de Gontaut-Biron, France;
Milton Vereide, The Philippines; and Minister of Justice
Edmond Michelet, France. Capital Photo Service

journalists complained they were too busy to get at the facts, and the public sometimes doesn't want the truth. This was frankly confessed and subsequently produced a wide-spread discussion in several French newspapers and intellectual journals. Nothing so convinced the I.C.L. leaders of the effectiveness of this conference approach as when Senator Brunhes arose to challenge one and all in the final moments of the conference and said, "No matter what our profession is, if a Christian cannot let the life of Christ be lived out through him and motivate every aspect of his life, then he has failed in his Christian vocation."

When Wallace Haines made his first visit to Holland as the guest of the Princess, Dr. Gaele van der Veen kindly offered to show him around. This initial contact developed into a great friendship and the ultimate appointment of Dr. van der Veen as special director for I.C.L. in Holland and technical organizer of the world conferences. Dr. van der Veen died suddenly in the United States in 1957 when visiting I.C.L. groups and his children, and Dr. Vereide, whom he loved devotedly as his spiritual father, was with him at the end.

In the spring of 1959, H.R.H. Princess Wilhelmina followed a suggestion to extend the hospitality of her palace of Het Loo for a week-end to responsible members of the Dutch I.C.L. About forty were invited including several Roman Catholics, by the Dutch Board who made all arrangements. The outstanding result of this Het Loo week-end was the new community of feeling among all the attendance, including the Roman Catholic men. Staunch conservative Calvinist Protestants found fellowship with these Catholic laymen. It was as if by being with one another in the name of Jesus Christ, He sent His Holy Spirit to draw all together. All left the week-end saying, "Only God could have brought us together in such a way." The new president, Mr. Jan Verhaar—a business man— rapidly followed up the spiritual unity of the Het Loo week-end and was soon able to report fifteen I.C.L. groups in The Netherlands.

Commenting on the "miracle of the Lord's unity at Het Loo," Mr. Haines added, "The purpose of I.C.L. is not to seek to bring Protestants and Catholics together, but to seek out men who are concerned about the problems of the day and who want the inspiration of Christ in unitedly undertaking their responsibilities. The question of one's denomination is not raised. Christian men are drawn together by the cohesive power of Christ's love and the moral and spiritual strength gained through fellowship."

Britain's first I.C.L. President was Ernest Williams, a civil engineer. His suggestion that a Victory Fellowship founded by him in England after World War II should amalgamate with I.C.L. was the start of I.C.L. overseas. Stanley Browne, a northern industrialist and tireless personal witness, General Peter Winser D. S. O., Colonel Harold Tapp M.C. who edited an I.C.L. magazine, Joan Pollock, widow of the late Bishop of Norwich, and the present President, James C. Young, J.P., who has a group of fifty in Newcastle, have all been active. John Cordle, M.P., speaking before President Eisenhower at the Annual Breakfast in 1959, made no secret of the centrality of his faith. He brought a message of greetings from his fellow countrymen, with warm memories and appreciation for the President's wartime leadership and moral integrity, also for the aid given by the nation to Britain in so many ways, but "best of all, you sent us in a very serious time of a grave vacuum after the war, spiritual help in the form of one of the best ambassadors, if I may say so with respect, America has ever had, in Dr. Billy Graham. He brought the glorious Gospel of Jesus Christ back again into our country, as we haven't had it for many a year. I stand here today as a living witness to the fact that it was through Billy Graham that I was brought to know Jesus Christ as my own personal Saviour. I had paid lip-service to church life. I realized after meeting Billy that Jesus Christ is a Person and a personal Saviour."

A long time member of the British Parliament courageously took the opportunity of Billy Graham's meetings in England and Scotland to assert his witness for Christ by rallying other members of parliament to the need of revival in Britain. Mr. John Henderson M.P., of Glasgow, formed an evangelical fellowship in Parliament after the Graham meetings. He acted as vice-president of international I.C.L. and often gave leadership to the conferences in Holland.

A. V., Wallace Haines and I.C.L. members of the Continent have realized that the English evangelical verve and balance are needed in international conferences, at which there have always been one or two spiritual leaders as speakers from England. Outstanding among these has been Canon Wallace Bird who left a profound impression several years in succession as the closing witness meeting at Nordwijk.

Germany also has a member of the Bundestag as its I.C.L. leader. Not many men talk like this, when they announce themselves as candidates for a Parliamentary election: "I told my constituency that I shall not say anything bad about the other fellow; that I shall not say anything bad about the other party; and that I shall not tell them what a real good fellow I am. I promised only that, if I am elected, I will stand in politics as a Christian." That was the election manifesto of Gustav-Adolph Gedat, the founder of I.C.L. in Germany, which won him his seat in the Bundestag. "Now," says he, "I have to live up to something—being a Christian in Parliament!"

Gus Gedat was already a well-known Christian leader. As National Y.M.C.A. secretary, he got into trouble with the Hitler regime through his best-selling book, *A Christian Facing the Problems of the World,* which sold 300,000 copies. After the war, he became one of the founders of the Christian Boys' Town Movement, helping thousands of homeless lads; and with young men and women from twelve nations he rebuilt the thousand-year-old castle in the Black forest, Burg Liebenzell, as a Christian training center. Under his leadership more than thirty I.C.L. groups are functioning in Germany today.

Probably the most significant work undertaken in Europe by I.C.L. has been the annual French-German conferences. One cannot imagine two civilized Christian nations more diverse in thinking and culture and more antagonistic until this postwar era. When dynamic Gus Gedat opened his magnificent international youth center at Burg Liebenzell, one of his first conferences was with French I.C.L. members. Germans had met French at the Noordwijk Conference in Holland. How would the French like to come to Germany?

Profuse words of greetings were spoken by the Germans in the opening sessions. Gracious hospitality was shown the French delegates. Each side observed the other. The little French Countess de Gontaut-Biron sat smiling and loving one and all, but her heart was praying. A distinguished political leader was brought from Bonn to make the grand impression of friendship. When he had finished his address, Senator Edmond Michelet spoke in sparkling but penetrating impromptu French fashion. He said he had attended international conferences on politics and on economics. He had come to this conference to find friendship in Christ and to help the Christian community of Europe. Immediately the distinguished leader from Bonn arose to reply: "I had not thought to hear a Frenchman speak in such a manner. Now I understand the reason for this conference. We need this Christian contact." It was the climax of the weekend. The little Countess looked across the room to Wallace. She was nodding her head and smiling the smile of victory and joy. The Spirit of God had come into the gathering. All were lifted from the human to the spiritual level. The German-French contact has continued with conferences each year, and the idea repeated in German-Dutch conferences.

All of the Nordic countries look to Stockholm as the center of a certain type of culture—not that all Nordic people follow Sweden in politics or ethics. The first concerted impact upon Scandinavia, which Norwegian-born Vereide wanted to see, was made with a Nordic conference at Stockholm in 1955. There were representatives from all four countries: Norway, Denmark, Finland and Sweden, with fraternal delegates from Germany, England, France and the United States. Senator Frank Carlson, whose mother tongue was Swedish, was pleased to come from Washington to preside.

Some two hundred took part. The Swedish prime minister spoke at a luncheon to emphasize that Christianity should have a larger effect on the political affairs of Sweden and other nations. The King's chamberlain was particularly moved. The magnificent closing service of praise in St. Jacob's Church was honored by the presence of Sweden's Archbishop. It was in this service that Vereide rose to prophetic heights in challenging the northern nations to return to the heritage of their fathers. His voice rang out through the vast church: "Righteousness exalteth a nation. Sin is a reproach to any people."

Carl Wahlquist, faithful colleague with Baroness Hermelin and the wife of Professor Sundberg, have been the ones to prepare potential meetings whenever the American team has come to Sweden, and now the first named is developing a vital men's group in Stockholm.

Finland, so close to Russia, has some of the strongest and most enthusiastic I.C.L. groups in Europe. Abram's impression is of "a Christian democracy which has in an amazing manner battled its way through seemingly insurmountable difficulties." He realized this when he visited Porkkala, the Finnish territory taken by the Russians and held for ten years, but now returned. "The devastated churches turned into dance halls," he said, "graveyards levelled and gravestones used for building purposes, stately buildings of former prosperous farms left filthy and demolished, were the mute evidences of the influence of a godless tyranny. This beautiful section of Finland was formerly populated by some 10,000 prosperous farmers." When meeting with members of Parliament, with four ministers of the government and the vice-speaker of Parliament present, "theirs was different from other Parliamentary groups," he said. "They sang hymns and entered into the session with a worshipful devotion and democratic participation which gripped me deeply. After my message they had many questions and comments."

A member of a visiting I.C.L. team, Rosalie Pretzfelder, commented on "the many wonderful things we discovered the Finnish people had been doing at home. The deep heart-searching to eradicate bitterness or resentment in their own lives, so that they might be able to let God's love pour through them to the needy Russians."

"No country in Europe so stirred my emotions by its courage, peace, and discipline," wrote Wallace Haines to Mr. Vereide. Haines had gone there with instructions from Abram to "seek out already existing movements and develop fraternal relations under an international council," for it was Vereide's world vision that God was everywhere raising up movements or groups of concerned men who visit to express this concern in international fellowship and action.

There in Finland Wallace Haines "discovered" Pavia Virkkunen and his team, Pentti Kaitero, Viljo Costren, Alli Wiherheimo, Max Eckholm, Aarne Hellemoa, Yrjo Massa and others, all intellectuals already formed in 1947 into the Society for Christian Culture.

"There is no more loyal circle of I.C.L. friends anywhere in the world than in Finland," Haines comments. "From the first world conference in 1952 which brought dynamic Ella Grönroos, and loving Werner Wiren and his charming wife, Sylvia, there has never been a conference without Finnish representation nor a year when some team has not visited Finland." Haines' annual visits have been remarkable for the heavy schedule of meetings, the widespread contacts and spiritual blessing. On one tour, fifteen cities were visited. Mr. Vereide was the honored guest at a Nordic I.C.L. conference held in Finland. There are now five groups orientated directly with I.C.L. The ladies' groups for prayer and Bible study under the direction of Sylvia Wiren have developed rapidly and were recently visited by Alicia Abrahamsen and Elizabeth Iglehart.

"Finland stands alone and unafraid between two parts of the world" is Haines' conclusion. "If she is free and prosperous, it is because here you find much deep piety which has its source in waves of revival, and these revival movements have been kept in the church. A communion service is marked with a deep fervor. A sermon is a Bible exposition. The bishops are men of the people, humble and devoted. Here is democracy and equality at its best. However, the parliamentary system stands in danger. Two I.C.L. men's groups, meeting in Helsinki, have the preservation of the country in peace and freedom. In one group, there is a cabinet minister, a bishop, a university professor, a leading industrialist, an internationally known scientist. What can one man do alone? In obedience to the command of the Lord—'where two or three are agreed as touching anything, there am I in the midst'—these leaders of modern Finland meet to pray and find strength in the fellowship of believers."

Europeans, however, are not just rubber stamps in adopting American ways. They often have as different an outlook from Americans in things Christian as in things political. The contrasts are healthy; each complements the other. Maybe Europe supplies the solidity and America the energy. On various occasions both the Dutch and the German committees of the I.C.L. sent words of warning and advice to Vereide and Wallace Haines.

Before one of the Noordwijk conferences Dr. Gaele van der Veen, who with Dr. Colijn, Gen. Calmeyer, Minister of External Affairs, Dr. Pieter Idenberg and others, formed a strong Dutch Committee, wrote on behalf of the Committee: "Our common opinion is that a movement such as I.C.L. can meet a need in life of many people, who have a deep hidden craving for a better life. If the I.C.L. will meet these needs, it has to be a real spiritual movement, where people will be confronted with an often unknown, but living Christ in whom life is in abundance. Many people do know a lot *about* Christ, but few have in these days a real experience of the living Christ. There are everywhere too many preachers who talk over the heads of people, but who do not really touch their hearts.

"The committee members have doubts whether all the speakers come up to the requirements of a spiritual movement as the I.C.L. should be and they have the impression— and they hope they are wrong—that a number of them are put on the program by virtue of their names or positions, but not by virtue of their spiritual Christian qualities. They would like to warn against symptoms of some kind of snobism, which they and others think to have diagnosed sometimes. 'It is not by might or power, but by the Spirit.'

"Our Committee is in full agreement with what one of our Scandinavian friends wrote on one of these days: 'I have been thinking on the Conference and what people need these days. I think that we must all be simple. It is not a question of a Christianity on a high intellectual level, which people can accept, although they do not have Christ in their hearts. We must show them Christ and give them the simple Gospel based on a personal *experience* with God Himself. We must be filled with His love, who suffered all for us.' "

Gus Gedat, on behalf of the German committee, wrote to Vereide: "The meeting of the German group leaders unanimously voted to call your attention to the following matter, asking you kindly to understand and to respect our attitude. We have learned that a great number of invitations for the Washington and the Noordwijk conferences has been sent to people who are on your mailing list. We all feel that for the sake of getting real and responsible representation of a national movement, the delegates should be elected by those who really know the movement and the people, that is, the national committee in each country. You know that particularly the relationship between Holland and Germany requires a German delegation as carefully selected as possible.

"We feel that the conference should work on concrete objects and should be very well prepared and that all addresses, lectures and speeches should betray mastery of the subject; they should be concise and to the point while the main work should be done in small working parties.

"We are particularly concerned that also the morning devotions should be solid and not a mere personal and emotional testimony. We call this in Europe 'Bible work.' You will remember that years ago we had already a discussion about this matter in Washington, and in my opinion it is interesting that our Dutch friends feel the same as we in Germany."

And even Wallace Haines, as he learned to sense the European outlook, wrote Vereide, "My dear Chief . . . I do beg you to underspeak about the spread or work of I.C.L. As our friends know us they question if we are so big or widespread as we appear to be. I have been asked several times, Is I.C.L. really established in this place or that? Europeans seem so afraid of American boasts or publicity."

Healthy antidotes!

To follow further present-day I.C.L. expansions, one needs an atlas. In 1959 a flying visit was made to India by Abram and Wallace Haines for the first I.C.L. conference in Madras. The pilot group in New Delhi had been initiated through the assistance of Dr. Melquiades J. Gamboa, the Ambassador from the Philippines and now her representative at the United Nations, who wrote: "I regard the International Christian Leadership as a fellowship of kindred spirits committed to Christ, that is non-sectarian, non-political and non-proselytizing. It is Christianity in depth because it seeks to touch the inner life of the individual in its totality. It is applied Christianity because it exhorts us to put into practice Christ's teaching in our daily life. The crisis of the world today being basically moral and spiritual, the power of Christ in the minds, hearts and wills of Christian leaders is the best hope, at this crucial time, that the free world can survive and have a sense of security. This the I.C.L. is trying to help bring about by making leaders of men who are God-guided and Christ-inspired."

This first conference in Madras was arranged by Clifton

Robinson, the leader of twenty groups in India. Dr. John Peters, president of World Neighbors, had just returned from India. He had been so impressed with the staggering need and tremendous opportunities, particularly for non-denominational groups like I.C.L. in which so much of leadership is centered, that he offered to take care of most of the expenses, if Abram would go.

It was a difficult decision to make because of health and other factors; but he had always longed to visit these countries on the other side of the world and, backed by his Executive Committee, he became increasingly certain that God was in this.

The first stop was in Paris for a reception at the Palace of Justice, with Minister Michelet as host. Subsequent stops and brief conferences in Rome, Athens, and Beirut "offered me," Abram wrote, "the opportunity of meeting for mutual counsel and rich Christian fellowship with men and women responsible for the work in these centers. Most challenging was the leadership in Athens under Professor Tsiritanes of Athens University."

A visit to the Holy Land, where he stayed in a guest house overlooking the Garden Tomb, gave him, he wrote, "the needed spiritual preparation for the rest of the journey. Jesus lives. He shall reign in us, through us and among us forever." He called it "the greatest experience of my life." Writing a note at dawn, he said, "Sitting over against the tomb of Jesus. There the body of Jesus lay. Just a stone's throw away on a hill they crucified my Lord. Here I am living that great event over again. It was all for me. My sins were buried with Him. Here He rose again. Mary and the other women, and Peter and John, came here and saw, and some believed while others doubted. Those who have doubted and rejected have gone into oblivion. The believers lived and made history."

Flying almost directly from the Garden Tomb to New Delhi, they were met at 4:30 A.M. at the airport by ten men of the I.C.L. group. "Such a warm welcome!" "No sooner had they arrived at the hotel room," Mrs. Clifton Robinson wrote Marian Johnson, "than Dr. V. gave them a message. He started off, 'Men, you know how much I love Jesus.' Several told me afterward how much it meant to them. That evening to a crowd of two hundred in the ballroom of the Imperial Hotel, Dr. V.

gave a stirring and moving address. We all knew that God was speaking through him to us. To every one he has met he has been a great blessing. As we waited at the new American Embassy to see Ambassador Bunker, it was a joy to hear him talk to our young Hindu guide. The witness he gave to this Indian man was underlined and emphasized by the shine on his face. Then he gave such a good word to the ambassador after a lovely chat, and closed the time with a brief, effective prayer."

Wallace Haines added his comments: "Cliff [Robinson] is doing an amazing job. He has plucked the fruit of a generation of missions. Most I.C.L. members are second generation. Cliff has glamor and dash and tremendous energy and can be kindness itself. He feels God was preparing him for I.C.L. back in the jungle! I admire his energy and his getting so many groups organized. God has led him to key men. He is like I am in enthusiasm for people—probably over-evaluating as I do. A.V., (as he is sometimes called) holds up amazingly. I have had two short anxious moments. He is so dear and wonderful and all God's—except his pushing a little too much. What an example for mystical Indians to see, who always love a holy man." And later he wrote, "What a man of God A.V. is. He is unrealistic at times—but he is filled with the Holy Spirit—so wonderful in personal work. I don't want to fail him or the Lord. Just to comfort A.V.—do all the little things—check him gently and learn from him. Have never been so aware that this is God's man!" And again: "I had a few minutes to remind him of his greatness—in reaching men for Christ and inspiring them: and of his weakness—not to train them and bring them on. I warned him he must train me more—that this trip had helped me to see him and feel him more than ever before. My plea—just build teamwork and thus create our sense of security in I.C.L. He owed it to us. He agreed. It is such a temptation to see myself as only a pigmy by the side of A.V. But the Lord wants me to see only Himself." And concerning finances, when the hotel bills were unexpectedly heavy: "I.C.L. has its financial struggles. There must be no illusions. A.V. feels such a responsibility—both money and time."

The parting at New Delhi reminded him, Abram said, of Paul's farewell to the Ephesian elders. The same welcome greeted them in Madras and Calcutta. "What a wonderful body of men they are!" he wrote. "Here is dedication, intelligence, experience and depth of spirituality manifest, the mind of Christ with the grasp of India's problems, and the realization that Jesus Christ and the application of His principles and teachings represent the solution everywhere."

Then came visits to I.C.L. forces in Hongkong, to his son Milton and Bonnie, his wife, dedicated Presbyterian missionaries teaching at the Bible School in Legaspi in the Philippines, with a large body of I.C.L. members in Manila, where "seeing and hearing what God is doing throughout these islands through the missionaries and nationals strengthened my faith and hope for the future"; to Okinawa where he was rushed to a meeting by the three sons of Lieut. General M. S. Silverthorn—a captain, a major and a colonel; to Japan, where representatives of Bob Pierce's World Vision and of Mr. Togasaki had arranged a full schedule, including a luncheon with members of Parliament and business and industrial leaders; and finally to Hawaii with Herbert Avery, General Silverthorn and many friends. Then he returned to Seattle, Washington, where the work had begun in 1935. "With renewed zeal and dedication," he wrote, "and with the arms of faith and love, I embrace every continent and the people of every class, color and creed with a fervent prayer that God will move upon men everywhere and raise up a leadership led by his Holy Spirit. His is the power, kingdom and glory forever!"

Commander Desta, the young grandson of the Emperor of Ethiopia, heads the I.C.L. group in Addis Ababa. Abram has the vision that this group can be the bridge from the old world to the new in Africa. Basil Photiades has maintained consistent contact with Washington and with Wallace Haines, leading a group in Istanbul where members of I.C.L. often stop for fellowship. Professor Tsirintanes is giving Bible studies in Athens which are used in professional men's groups. He has several times been a speaker at Noordwijk. As an inspired, creative thinker of modern Greece and author of *Toward a Christian Civilization,* he has made a substantial contribution to the ideology of world I.C.L., as well as guiding the renewed spiritual-life movement among the intellectuals of Greece, together with his "alter ego," the saintly Royal Chaplain, Father

Jerome Cotsonis. Professor Burton Thurston of the American University in Beirut felt the need of an international prayer group and, inspired by I.C.L., has now gathered a small group around him.

In a conference held in Mexico City, Professor Gustavo Velasco said, "I feel that International Christian Leadership is breaking down barriers and bringing us together into one family unit in Jesus Christ our Lord and Saviour. When will the time come for my country and other countries in Latin America to have Christian men in key positions in government offices and in business, ready to lead their Christian lives?"

President Figueras of Costa Rica invited Mr. Vereide for a series of meetings in San José, beginning with a reception at the palace and the conference sessions in the National Theater, broadcast on both the Catholic and Protestant radio. At the final banquet Abram spoke on Christ "the Clue and Climax of history." As he left, he wrote back to his wife, "In the midst of beautiful scenery and the feeling of timelessness, there is the melodrama of human suffering and discord. I have listened to these stories and looked at men and women created by God and for God, but blinded to beauty, purpose, plan and the eternal prospects. My heart yearns for them as I seek to open their eyes and point them to the Light of the world. What a contrast between a man who is still away from Him and the man who has become a new man in Him!"

22 | AFRICA'S YEAR OF DESTINY

The need of Africa in its year of destiny, 1960, with its upsurge of new leaders and new nations, weighed so heavily on Wallace Haines that he wrote A.V. to say he felt compelled to make a tour of the African continent, even though he had not the money for his ticket. He was just going to book in faith and go, which he did.

But when Abram learned of this stirring in Wallace's heart, he announced to his intimates that he was going to find the necessary money for him. He set out on one of his frequent long journeys—this time to contact a wealthy consecrated layman on behalf of Wallace and to seek a speaker for the annual Presidential Breakfast in Washington. In the meantime, an I.C.L. friend who believes in Wallace's mission in Europe sent him a substantial sum the day his ticket was due. This was not enough to cover such an extensive four months' tour, but just at the right moment, when Wallace had already started, Abram was able to send a larger sum to cover all expenses.

Daily in his traveling through Africa, Wallace said he keenly felt the backing of Abram—his prayers, his faith, his ideals. Often would he think, How would A.V. handle this situation? How would he approach this man? Africans recognize a prophet, and it always stirred their interest when Wallace told of this "great-hearted man of God in Washington," who loved men everywhere, because in his humble youth he gave his heart and life to the Lord Jesus Christ; and how God had taken this man, His man now grown to be a prophet, to be His witness in the presence of presidents, kings, queens, and national leaders.

The visits were brief, to sixteen countries, but it opened the doors. He was witnessing the birth of the new Africa. He returned with the conviction that I.C.L. never had a greater challenge and responsibility than this—to reach the leadership of these new nations for Christ.

Algeria was the first stop. Sen. Michelet had given him introductions, enabling him to catch the spirit of the French in that boiling cauldron. Mingling with the French, he naturally caught the French point of view, though at its best, rather than that of the Algerian nationalists. He found among them a hope of some French-Algerian amalgamation, vain hope in this present tidal wave of independence. He and his French traveling companion, Marcel Bresard, were particularly impressed by the French officials. "We met men, not functionnaires," he said. "Whether government, military or ordinary citizens, they have a sense of dedication to a mission." In Gen. Faure, the Commander in Chief, he found "one of the finest men I ever hope to meet. No wonder he is given the delicate job of general, father and democratizer. He is a clear thinker." "We have an important moral mission," said the General.

"We work at the creation of a life, not the defense of a way of life."

The Director of the cabinet in Oran finely stated to Wallace, "Algeria is not a tragedy but a challenge. It is at the same time France's cross but also her great opportunity." Pastor Andre Chaloney, head of all French Protestant work, said that they must find a way to cooperate. "To create a man amalgamated is a necessity," was his comment; and that since De Gaulle had taken charge, there was hope for a new future, Arab and European becoming united: "A phenomenon, a ferveur collective," he called it. But the Rev. Hans Aurbackken, a Norwegian and head of the Methodist church in Algeria gave the Christian answer: "Only Christianity is capable of a sound integration. Islam is a community held together by law without an interior change. Therefore there is no freedom in Islam."

On arriving in Dakar, Senegal, Wallace noted the "conscious, deliberate, severe, black airport officials, a new day dawning in the Mali Federation. He met two African members of the cabinet who were Christians and open to I.C.L. ideals, though the great majority of the people are Moslem. He attended a service in the mountains of the interior which was unforgettable, with a small mixed French-African congregation, a Protestant service led by a young pastor and held in the Roman Catholic chapel of the army with 'the Holy Virgin illuminated in her niche above. The service was rich in Bible reading and the singing of the congregation vigorous. In our smallness and loneliness we desperately wanted to know that He was real. It was the church of Jesus Christ that night at Thies.' I envision a small, strategic Protestant-Catholic group in Dakar," he said.

A short stay in Sierra Leone, a little country preparing for independence, was encouraging. The Governor, Sir Maurice Dorman, a truly Christian man keen on vital Christianity, was very much interested in I.C.L. Wallace found no British pride or antipathy there. He believes the colony will become the Switzerland of West Africa in stability, culture and thrift, and that the transformation to independence will be easy. A Fellowship Group with leaders is planned. "I am humbled before God when I realize I am experiencing the emergence of these small countries."

In Monrovia, Liberia he found in Prof. Frank Tichy, American professor of biology at the University of Liberia, a potential leader for I.C.L., and in meetings with Liberian leaders, including the Vice-President, he was encouraged by cabinet members to return. A visit to a missionary of the Worldwide Evangelization Crusade, an old friend, took him to a gospel service in a pagan village deep in the bush. "The missionaries begged me to return for Bible conferences, but my mission in Africa is souls and I.C.L. I can see I.C.L. calling out leaders in every nation on earth—leaders led by God, committed to Christ, before our Lord comes. I thank God for this new development of I.C.L. in Africa. The missionaries are so pleased we are tackling leaders."

Some countries had to be regretfully by-passed. He addressed sixty leaders in Ghana and gave the challenge for "laymen to witness and form Fellowship Groups as the new line of evangelism and outreach for the Church."

The Chief Magistrate in Lagos, Nigeria, with whom Wallace had fellowship and prayer, was greatly concerned about graft in Government and the overwhelming Moslem vote in the north. He saw the need of "a strategic fellowship to pray, and plans to start one." Wallace was seeing more clearly all the time the call of God to I.C.L. to "bring into existence in these newer nations strategic fellowship groups to pray for the nation and bring cleansing in high office and national life." "We have a brief time of opportunity in this area," he wrote from Nigeria. "Most of the new states are secular in the extreme, with constitutions and lip service to religious freedom. Christianity must be stripped of any foreign trade mark."

Over on the east coast in Kenya he found optimism. The Bishop said the good word: "Praise God for the opportunity for the Church now to preach Christ and not the Christian culture of the West." One African he found in Kenya stood out in political circles for his Christian testimony, Musa L. Amalemba, M.P. and a member of the Cabinet. As a speaker at the 1960 International Conference in Holland, it was Amalemba's message at the Ridderzaal meeting, in its intensity and reality, which peculiarly moved the audience.

In Rhodesia, and South Africa young National Party M.P.'s, whom Wallace contacted and addressed, were impressed by

I.C.L. and felt it would be welcome and useful as being, "Christ-centered and evangelical; non-political; non-critical, but bridge-building; working quietly and without undue publicity."

The Congo Wallace found most disturbing with independence then drawing near. "All say, come—hurry! All say with one voice, 'Africa needs Christian leaders.' The undertow of debasing influences is so evident. It means—to find the best men, make contact, draw them together and let the Lord change and cleanse their personal lives. Materialism is not the answer."

Crossing the southern border into Rhodesia for the Billy Graham meeting, he saw a microcosm, as it were, of the opposing forces; "the conflict, the victory, and yet the continuing reality of indifference and contempt of the truth of God, which rules out any slackening or complacency in Christian witnessing. The meeting began with 'Vive l'Independence' and tear gas. It ended with 'Vive Christ' and His Gospel and tears of repentance."

But, sitting among the English at the mass meeting, though there was no planned segregation, he was surprised and disturbed at some of the restiveness. "The smoking disturbed me. The whispering and moving about was unsportsmanlike. It seems that the English, something like the Americans, when uprooted and abroad, can be undisciplined and pagan. The prayer of the missionaries is for Christian leadership among the Africans. The need of the white settlers and business men is everywhere apparent—to the extent that in some places they seemed the neglected heathen. It may be that the Billy Graham meetings have stirred two kinds of Europeans in Africa: those who never go to church, but went to a sports arena where they became aware of the claims of the Gospel, but took no step. Also those Christian laymen committed to Christ but doing nothing about it. Some reacted to Billy Graham's meetings thus: if this American team is so stirred to win men to Christ and have these results, why am I not reaching some?"

Wallace's last visit gave him in complete form and actual practice the answer—God's answer—for Africa. He visited an area of central Africa where the Spirit of God has been at work among Africans and Europeans for a number of years, in Ruanda-Urundi and surrounding regions.

"This spiritual life movement has been under way for twenty years," he wrote. "Africans and a few whites meet weekly in various centers for testimony and praise and confession of need. It was in this fellowship that I came to realize the true oneness in Christ possible between African and white.

"The simplicity of expression, the freedom to share one's needs and victories, and the kind corrections and admonitions to discipline, made me greatly aware of the Holy Spirit's flow through lives given over to Him. 'Jesus' was upon the lips of everyone who spoke in these fellowship meetings. Just walking with Jesus and loving Him seemed the normal Christian way. Not that this was always the case or easy, because there was another word much heard in the testimony— *repentance*. A senior missionary confessed to coldness. He had repented of this and knew the cleansing of the blood of Christ. A black brother had repented of always looking for things wrong in the lives of the white missionaries. He testified that Jesus had forgiven him. The brothers in Nairobi could thank the Lord for the political ferment, calling it the work of Satan and causing Christians to see that what mattered most was having Jesus.

"What I saw was that these revival Christians were simply walking in the light of Jesus—letting His Spirit check any false move or wrong attitude, and coming immediately to the blood of Jesus for cleansing (1 John 1:7). This was a daily, hourly experience.

"A whole chain of sins, failures and difficulties in my life were marched right up to His blood in that afternoon meeting as the light from Jesus showed what sins or failures there were which needed to be confessed to Him, repented of and deliberately and literally brought to the blood for cleansing and forgiveness.

"The African has a subtle way of getting a point across by inference. An African archdeacon of a large district paid me a visit. He humbly told of his visit to the Pan-Angelican Conference in the United States. I asked him if he gave a clear witness to Jesus Christ before such an august body. He told me he twice preached in the Cathedral of St. John the Divine. Again

I complimented him, but rather patronizingly asked him if he could give his true witness to Christ there. His response was that he had a D.D. degree—Down in the Dust at the feet of Jesus. I was so taken aback, I could only bow my head in shame and laugh in my embarrassment. This African clergyman knew the American preachers' love for degrees, for the impression of dignity and scholarship. He also sensed my patronizing air— the mere curiosity I had in his speaking in the proud cathedral of New York. For a long time afterwards I asked the Lord to give me His D.D. like our African brother—Down in the Dust at the feet of Jesus."

Summing up the tour as he turned homeward, he wrote, "I do believe in I.C.L. It is so clear and compelling in my mind. It has a mission in the world, if its leaders avoid extremism of doctrine or politics and remain warmly evangelical and Christ-centered, is converted, dynamic laymen reaching out to nominal laymen, drawing them into a fellowship and experience where they discover what they have missed and really want, down underneath all the indifference. I find it much easier to put it across out here and no one says no—even if it is wholly new."

23 | A VISIT TO DR. SCHWEITZER

Wallace only took time on the tour for one special visit outside the course of his normal activities. It was to Dr. Albert Schweitzer. He sent a special letter describing the visit to his two sons, Philip and Stephen, who had asked their father to promise to visit the doctor and his hospital: "*February* 20, 1960. When I finally arrived in the midst of the jungle of Gabon yesterday afternoon, no one met me at the crude airport (the letter announcing his visit had not got through). No one could give me advice. I was tempted to enter the airplane again and continue to Brazzaville. No telephone to Dr. Schweitzer and no electricity.

"I sat on the veranda of the hotel and thought I was in the Garden of Eden—primitive and primordial—luxurious jungle, the wide river, the distant hills and the many clouds. For two hours I sat there and meditated. Then the tourists came back from a trip and jazz music and the drinking began. The white man takes discontent, unconcern and sin wherever he goes.

"When morning came, the hotel owner sent me to Dr. Schweitzer by motor boat. Immediately I entered into quiet and peace and fellowship. The old doctor was loading lumber into a boat at the shore. What a kindly (even saintly) smile of welcome he gave me. He is 85 years old and always he must work. Sister Mathilde received me in exquisite French style. A German doctor from Munich showed me round the whole estate. I became faint and almost sick when I saw the patients with leprosy. This is a small village (not a big building) for sick people. The doctors were operating when I arrived. Dr. Schweitzer was supervising construction. Everybody was busy. All who stay here must work. Dr. Schweitzer is a strong leader. He expects obedience. The natives must be taught to work.

"At lunch I sat across the table from the great doctor. The French nurse sat on one side of him and the Dutch nurse on the other. Swiss girls do the cooking. I told him about you boys and our wonderful French friends. We had five different kinds of fruits at lunch. I believe Dr. Schweitzer does not eat meat, but we were served meat. He spoke at the table about the horrors of war. He suffers very much about war and fears the new struggle between African countries. My doctor friend from Munich reminded me that Christ has overcome the world and we must be in Christ. He quoted R. Tagore of India: 'The end of anxiety is the beginning of being.'

"I have now met a nurse from the Union of South Africa, a Sudeten German Jewish doctor, an elegant doctor from Argentina, a doctor from Vienna, a young Canadian doing construction work, and a rich American who has three times tried to take his life and says he believes in nothing. All here are sorry Dr. Billy Graham and his party were not able to stop off for a visit. Dr. Schweitzer is genuinely catholic in love and understanding. Many Roman Catholics come to his hospital when sick. A Catholic Mother Superior with a beautiful face is now a patient. Dr. Schweitzer belongs to all.

"There are many pet animals from the forest here near his cottage. I have taken pictures for you of his pets: a gorilla, a chimpanzee, a pelican, dogs, a wildcat, deer, owls, etc. Dr. Schweitzer loves all living things. He will not kill any living animal. All are well cared for. I have been watching him playing just now with his pets. It is amusing to see the pelican tease the chimpanzee. If the chimpanzee gets too much, he covers himself with a cloth, just like some church people who cover themselves with religiosity when they can't face the world.

"I do not agree with Dr. Schweitzer's theology. I do not understand his philosophy. One seldom addresses him. He is authoritarian but benevolent. He is a man apart with no interest in petty things—only the big broad philosophy of life, the need to set the example by work and character before the Africans, and above all to do one's duty. One feels he is thoroughly aware of God and unafraid. Tonight he played a hymn on his famous piano and read in German, St. Luke 7:19-22. After this he took me aside to talk with me. One thing stands out: 'I don't ask, Is this or that the will of God, as modern theologians do. I simply ask myself what would Jesus do or what would Jesus say.'

"This morning Dr. Schweitzer took me to his bedroom for a long talk. He had food on a paper on his desk so the ants could come and eat. He told me laughingly that it was a restaurant for the ants. He told me about the revelation God gave him one day on the river which gave him the concept: reverence for life. He gave me autographed pictures of himself for each of you boys. Dr. S. wants you to love all living things and never be cruel to any animal, insect or human being, since God created all life and Christ puts the love of good in you."

24 | CO-WORKERS IN PLENTY

To many readers who do not know I.C.L. on the inside, the mention of different ones who had a vital part in the work will not be of special interest. But some should be mentioned. A mere sight of the names and positions held by many of their owners may indicate the readiness of so many to be identified with a definite Christian movement.

It would also be very wrong to leave the impression that I.C.L. is a one-man activity and that when Abram goes, it goes with him, even though this book concentrates largely on him. There is also the problem of mentioning some and, among all who have had contacts with I.C.L. overlooking others. To these latter we must apologize.

Naturally Abram's thoughts go back to the foundation members in Seattle, the birthplace of I.C.L. That first group originally consisted exclusively of presidents of companies, because of the influence they would have by their Christian witness; but as they began to be concerned for their junior executives and others, the group began to be enlarged. Some of these early members were William St. Clair, president of the Frederick Nelson Department Store, the largest department store west of Chicago, and the first president of the Breakfast Group; Chief Justice Matthew Hill; Arthur B. Langlie, the former governor of the state; Winfield Langlie, his brother; Mayor William Devin; F. A. Ernst, president of the Ernst Hardware Company, who succeeded St. Clair as president of the Breakfast Group; James F. Pollard, president of the Seattle Gas Company; A. W. Hogue, senior vice-president of the Pacific National Bank; Admiral C. S. Freeman; Harvey Swanson, president of the Sweden Freezer Company, who found Christ through the Breakfast Group; Warren Dewer, a leading attorney brought to Christ through the Breakfast Group and who made great sacrifices for Christ's sake, giving up profitable practices which weren't in line with his Christian principles, and freely giving legal help to many Christian organizations.

From Vancouver to Southern California, Abram "cannot begin to mention the men in so many cities who were converted and began to exercise a Christian witness"—a big lumber man here, an automobile dealer there, and so on.

In Chicago, the next main center of I.C.L. there were Orlo Montague, president of a large realtor company; William Beaudry, president of Beaudry Landscape Architects; James Cunningham, president of Republic Flow Meter Company; Harold Benson, head of Benson Tailoring Company; and Victor

Van Kamp, president of Van Kamp Banking Firm; Congressman Frederick Busby, an active leader in Chicago as well as in the House of Representatives Group.

In the House of Representatives, among early members, foundation men were Karl Stefan of Nebraska, Paul Cunningham of Iowa, John Sparkman (now Senator) of Alabama, Gerald Bryson of South Carolina; Knute Hill of Washington and Russ Rizley of Oklahoma. Others through recent years who have taken the leading part in the House Groups are Walter Judd of Minnesota, Brooks Hays of Arkansas for years a vice-president of I.C.L., Charles A. Bennett of Florida, Katharine St. George of New York, Alvin Bentley of Michigan who was shot by a radical Puerto Rican and gave testimony at the Presidential Breakfast that his life was preserved through prayer.

Faithful in the Senate Group have been Senators Alexander Wiley of Wisconsin, Ralph Flanders of New Hampshire, A. Willis Robertson of Virginia, Frank Carlson of Kansas, Alexander Smith of New Jersey, John Stennis of Mississippi, Hawkes of New Jersey, Stuart Symington of Missouri, Price Daniel (now Governor) of Texas.

Of the armed services, Lieut. Gen. Willard S. Paul, now president of Gettysburg College, was an I.C.L. president; Lieut. Gen. Milton Silverthorn of the Marines, who recently found a living faith through I.C.L., has taken his witness to Christ to several lands; Gen. Robert Porter, head of personnel in the Pentagon, was a great helper in the active I.C.L. group in Frankfurt, Germany; Gen. Thomas Lane, Commissioner of the District of Columbia, got leave from his duties to accompany Abram to Mexico to establish the witness there and, as he termed it, "to carry A.V.'s bag." Rear Admiral Robert Morris was a member of the recent I.C.L. visiting team to Europe; he committed his life to Christ two years ago after a lady had spoken to him on a railway journey. Lieut. Gen. Clovis E. Byers, former chief of staff of NATO was active in the French group and now in Washington.

In New York the Breakfast Group was started by Thomas Watson, president of International Business Machines. Ernest Inwood, director of research in the Railroad Express Company, is co-ordinator of the New York groups. Admiral C. S. Freeman, formerly with A.V. on the West Coast, initiated the Princeton Club luncheon group.

One of three men who put in many hours of work as treasurer of I.C.L. was Donald Stone, who received much spiritual quickening through I.C.L. He was Assistant Director of the Bureau of the Budget and Deputy Director of the I.C.A. (commonly called the Marshall Plan) and gave hours to help in the program and budget of I.C.L., often coming in late at night, tired after a grueling day, to take his part in planning and discussion. When visiting Athens as deputy director of I.C.A. and taken, at his request, to visit Mars Hill, he opened his New Testament and read Paul's speech accompanied by his own testimony to the officials who escorted him.

When he went to another appointment, Ed Wilbur, Director of the Budget of the Department of State, who found Christ through I.C.L., was an equally indefatigable worker as I.C.L. treasurer. Nathan Bushnell, a Prudential Insurance agent, was changed from being a scoffer who went to church occasionally to pull the preacher to pieces, to a devoted Episcopalian and a Christian witness, who, after Ed Wilbur, devoted himself to the work and to assisting Abram in the early years, along with Col. Harold Folk of the World Bank.

Like the writer to the Hebrews, "time would fail me to tell" of so many men who have given of themselves in various ways to the work, and naturally those in touch with the center at Fellowship House come more easily to mind than those in other cities and countries. Ed Cabaniss, president of Joseph Dixon Crucible Company of New Jersey, served as president of I.C.L. for several years; the Right Hon. Norman Makin, Australian Ambassador to the U.S., was an early president; Senator Ralph Flanders was another president in early days and was of inestimable assistance to A.V., as was Senator Price Daniel until he went to be Governor of Texas; Frank Fuhr, a former pilot who met Christ when his plane was at a great altitude, was assistant to Mr. Vereide; Bob Doing of the New York Telephone Company edited the *Bulletin* for a time. The great change in his life, partly through I.C.L. and partly through Alcoholics Anonymous, has resulted in his giving his life as a witness to Christ as a lay evangelist in the Episcopal Church. Maribel Mears, deeply centered in Christ after a radical conversion from

*A **Training** Weekend in Fellowship House, Washington, with men from 13 States. The four men standing in the center are (l. to r.) Dr. Dick Halverson, Judge Homer Ferguson, Abraham Vereide and Gen. Silverthorn. Judge Boyd Leedom, President of I.C.L., is second from right, kneeling.*

The Dining Room, Fellowship House, Ambassadors' Luncheon: Seated (l. to r.) Judge Boyd Leedom, Dr. Abraham Vereide, Mrs. David Swanson, George Powell, H. E. Dr. Juan Plate, Paraguay; Roy Cooke, Judge Homer Ferguson, H. E. Dr. Celeo Davila, Honduras. Standing, l. to r.—Hon. Stanley Hornbeck, Douglas Coe, Mrs. Vereide, William Bullard, Minister Carlo Perrone Capano, Italy; First Sec. R. M. Akwei, Ghana; Dr. You Chan Yang, H. E. Ernest Bonhomme, Haiti; Counselor G.D.L. White M.V.D., New Zealand; H. E. Sheikh Abdullah Al-Khayyal, Saudi Arabia; H.E. George K.C. Yeh, China; Minister Kwang Lim Koh, Korea.   Capital Photo Service, Inc.

a pagan life, commuted from Philadelphia for several years to edit the *Bulletin*. Richmond Roberts expended himself in love and devotion for years ministering to the Washington groups. Bob Pierce of World Vision, who is doing remarkable work in taking visiting teams to hold revival conferences with many hundreds of ministers in the lands of the younger churches, has always been a close friend, speaker, and practical helper in I.C.L. Corrie ten Boom goes around the world with her vibrant witness of the way the Lord met her when in the hands of the Germans in Holland. She was first introduced to the American public by Abram. Edwin Orr is also a world traveler, author, and evangelist.

Others are:

Al Graunke, a group leader and garage proprietor who mends lives as much as cars; George Gardner, an automobile dealer; Mrs. Rosella Pretzfelder, a faithful teammate at home and abroad; Mel Nelson; Bill Pringle; George and Kay Roberts, leaders in the Philadelphia area, and who initiated the work in Bermuda; Justice Charles A. Loreto, whose wife, the former Rosalie Leslie, was mentioned above as Assistant Dean of Women at the University of Maryland.

Dr. Gamboa and Sir Claude Corea have been outstanding in their witness to Christ as foreign ambassadors in Washington and the United Nations. Dr. Gamboa was chairman of the I.C.L. diplomatic group when with the Philippine Embassy in Washington. Sir Claude Corea, Ambassador for Ceylon and chairman of the Asia-Africa committee of the U.N., has been I.C.L. representative in the United Nations and a faithful witness to Christ.

Judge Boyd Leedom, chairman of the National Labor Relations Board and present president of I.C.L., found the inner certainty of Christ two years ago through the group at Fellowship House. He gives a leadership to I.C.L. which has the heart-warming quality of personal conviction. Judge Homer Ferguson, former Senator and Ambassador to the Philippines where he was the founder of the Breakfast Group, and now Chief Justice of the Court of Military Appeals, has been one of Abram's most faithful supporters, as has Dr. Ernest Griffiths of the Library of Congress. Senator Frank Carlson of Kansas, as president of I.C.L. International, was responsible for first inviting his friend, President Eisenhower, to attend the annual prayer breakfast, and he has

Dr. Vereide with the Hon. George
E. Hayes, District Commissioner,
Washington, D.C., 1960.

Dr. Vereide in Fellowship House
Garden in 1957, at 70.

*Conference in Garden of Fellowship House: standing on
r., Frank S. Weitzel, Dep. Comptroller General of U.S.A.;
standing on l., Dr. John Evans; front row, kneeling on r.,
Dr. Richard C. Halverson, Dr. Melvin Casberg, Chief of
Medical Forces of Defense Dept.; Hon. Katharine St.
George; Hon. Charles E. Bennett; on l., Wallace Haines,
Mrs. Vereide; A. Vereide in front.*

visited various countries to preside over I.C.L. conferences. Jim
Bell, a Washington attorney and secretary of I.C.L. in Washington, and Paul Temple of the Standard Oil Company, are
younger men vitally interested and active in I.C.L. Justin Edger-
ton, president of the Washington Bar, is attorney for I.C.L., and
Justin Williams, an executive in the I.C.A., has been ICL treasurer and is now assisting the work in France. Attorney James
Sherier gave many hours in the early days of Fellowship House.

Active also in I.C.L. in Washington are Bradshaw Mintner,
an attorney and formerly Assistant Secretary of the Department
of Health, Education, and Welfare; John Sumter, official of the
American Trust and Security Company; Judge George Powell,
a trial examiner of the National Labor Relations Board; John
Broger, Deputy Director of Information and Education of the
Department of Defense; Dr. Elgin Grosclose, an economist and
author of many books, who re-established the economy and
banking system of Iran.

Finally, as we move into the center with Abram and Mrs.
Vereide and Alicia, there is Dick Halverson, Associate Executive Director of I.C.L. and Abram's right hand. Dick, who before conversion was going into the show business, became
assistant minister at the Hollywood Presbyterian Church and
chaplain to the Hollywood Christian Fellowship, an affiliate of
I.C.L. which maintains a witness to Christ among the actors
and actresses and those connected with the movie world. Although now minister of the Fourth Presbyterian Church of
Washington, Dick Halverson gives much of his time to I.C.L.
affairs and is a magnificent speaker, particularly to men; as a
wise and balanced administrator and as one who can mix
with and reach those who are the special objective of I.C.L.,
he makes a God-given second to Abraham Vereide.

With Dick Halverson, and of the younger generation, is
Douglas Coe. Along with Bill Bullard and several others of his
co-workers who have accompanied him, Doug Coe is God's
latest gift to I.C.L. A young man, he had for some years been
active in the Navigators work, especially on the campus in the
state of Oregon and in bringing up young Christians in the
faith by an original method of Scripture memorization. Doug
was helpful in the development of the spiritual life of Mark
Hatfield, the young governor of Oregon. Doug has found in
I.C.L. the breadth of opportunity and greatness of vision for

which God had been preparing him. Bill Bullard, who has the gift of attending to detail and has been Editor of the I.C.L. Bulletin, was brought up with no religious training but was converted from a godless life in the Navy. These two, in their discipleship training of the key men in each group in Washington, have evoked an enthusiastic response and are meeting a long-standing need for a more thorough training and a continuing chain reaction in Christian commitment. This they combine with all they learn from their close contacts with A.V. As Doug says, "Dr. Vereide is the greatest personal worker I have ever known."

There is no respect of jobs with God any more than there is of persons, and to mention last is not to mean least the staff workers in home and office, who have made the wheels of hospitality and organization go round. Office workers have been many these twenty-five years: Carrie Lee White, now the wife of Dr. J. Braden Thompson of Boston, outstanding as a prayer partner and A.V.'s personal secretary for seven years; Margot Amies of England, who felt called to give her life to gospel work in France; Adrienne Sanders, faithful bookkeeper; and the present secretarial staff, Ann Lawler, Ruth Ludwig and Marilyn Isaac; and in Fellowship House, Emily Stiles, who has given many years of long service to Marian Johnson and to all comers at the headquarters.

And all these do not mention the Breakfast Group leaders, financial supporters, and witnessing members past and present, scattered through the cities of this country—like a mighty army. . . .

* * * * * *

Abram and Mattie Vereide celebrated their fiftieth wedding anniversary on August 27th, 1960. Quite an occasion was made of it by friends in Washington. Maribel Mears wrote in a personal letter to Marian Johnson who was on a visit to Europe: "I went to D.C. last Friday evening for the big event. Mr. Vereide asked what all this was about—so much to-do about an anniversary. But I am sure he was pleased. The response was overwhelming. Cards, cables, telegrams, flowers, gifts and people. The hall at the Church of the Pilgrims was beautiful. There were almost two hundred there. Congress was in session and the men could not get away, but some of the wives were there. When the people had got through the receiving line,

Golden wedding family group 1960. (l. to r.) John Abrahamsen (grandson) and wife, Tom McMurray (with daughter Karen), Gretha McMurray (granddaughter), Martha Vereide, Abe Vereide Jr. (with Kevin Abram), Alicia Abrahamsen, and Sharon Vereide with her grandparents, Mr. and Mrs. Abraham Vereide.

Judge Boyd Leedom, who presided, asked Dr. Taylor to offer a prayer. Then he introduced those who made the presentations of the three gifts of money, one for Abram, one for Fellowship House, and one for I.C.L. Before Abram acknowledged them he asked Fague Springman to sing "Amazing Grace." Then Mattie gave a speech which as usual brought a great response. Alicia read a poem that was exceedingly clever and gave a few words based on Genesis 18:19. She looked beautiful and was carrying a great responsibility as usual. Mattie was radiant, Abram up to the occasion of course. This was my first fiftieth wedding celebration. It was a great occasion to see these two so precious to me in this distinguised role."

Mrs. Vereide herself added this in a letter to Marian Johnson: "The church hall looked beautiful, large gold displays of 50 years. The biggest surprise to us was our two large wedding photos from Seattle, also our wedding certificate in large gold frame, and many of our old pictures in our youth, all placed in a large display beautifully done by an artist friend of Alicia's. The table looked beautiful. Marion Adair and others really put much work into this—a very large wedding cake, coffee, sandwiches, etc. Jim Bell spoke on behalf of Fellowship House, and Judge Ferguson on behalf of groups on the Hill (Senate and House of Representatives) and presented Abram with fifty $50 dollar bills. We received over fifty telegrams of congratulations and over a hundred cards (beautiful). We received several pieces of gold plate and gifts of money, but what we are most thankful for is friends. We felt so rich surrounded with so much love shown us and expressed appreciation for our work—all the glory goes to God."

Abram's daughter, Alicia, accompanied her father on a visit to his homeland after the 1960 Nordwijk Conference. It was a heart stirring experience for her.

"Coming into the small harbor of Moldoy at the entrance of Nordfjord, to see the typical Norwegian homes nestled on the hillside and to see a group of people waiting on the dock and to know that some of them were my relatives was thrilling.

"In a short while as the boat came nearer to the dock, we were calling out, 'Aunt Karen, Uncle Hans' and there was a waving of hands. Moldoy is the home of Abraham's only living sister. Even though she was 81 years old, she was still tall and erect, with lovely gray hair. Her eyes were so clear, and her coloring youthful. You could detect immediately here was a woman whose life had been lived to the fullest for the Lord. She had warmth, insight and understanding. She could not speak English, but that wasn't necessary as she welcomed the Americans and the man from India, Mr. Paul Parker. She knew the universal language of love.

"It was an unforgettable sight as Dad and I stood outside the old State church in Vereide to see there relatives, near and distant, and friends driving down the narrow country road along the fjord or coming by boat or walking down the hill on a winding path. The church on Sunday morning was soon packed and many of the women and children wore their national costumes which made a colorful sight.

"Dad brought a warm message in Norwegian and surprised his people by the beautiful Norwegian he was able to speak after so many years of not using his native tongue. He stepped down from the high pulpit and called on the friends from America to share their Christian experience.

"I shall never forget the thrill I had to be with my father in his homeland and to see him in the church where he was baptized and to see him with his sister's children and distant cousins of whom I had heard so much since early childhood. Here I was, seeing Dad breathing in the invigorating mountain air, gazing upon the lofty snow-covered mountains all around him and the rocks which he had always liked to climb, passing the appreciation on to us. I could see in those eyes the dreams, the hopes, the lofty ideals that had become a part of him as a young boy living in such majestic surroundings. Now he had returned, his dreams realized. Big mountains of discouragement hadn't turned him aside from his vision which God gave him. A land had been conquered for Christ, roots dug, mountains scaled. He had stumbled over the stones sometimes, but he quickly recognized the enemy and came up again with his vision beyond, leaving evidences in America of a man of daring faith such as the Vikings of old.

"I learned in Vereide that Dad had always had a ruggedness, a desire to explore beyond the mountains, to venture forth and to dare new things because of an early conception of the greatness of God and that with Him nothing is impossible.

"As I stood in that church that day to share with those precious people what was in my heart I couldn't speak for I just filled up with emotion. But more than that, it was an overflowing sense of God's grace. I stood there that morning because of nothing I did, but because of my grandmother and great-grandmother who had prayed and dedicated their children and grandchildren to the Lord. I heard stories of their great faith and their influence up and down the fjord. I was told about one aunt who, during the week, snow or ice, rain or sunshine, would row to small villages and homes to conduct a Bible study or prayer meeting and to share Christ with everyone. She had a vision, too, of reaching people for Him. Her picture still hangs on many a wall because of the appreciation people have for her and her life. As I stood before those villagers that morning, with oceans of God's love and mercy flooding me, I couldn't speak because of the great sense of the grace of God. It was a refining process in my own life. I recalled the verse in Genesis 18:19 where God tells Abraham, "I know thee, Abraham, that thou wilt command thy children after me" and right there I rededicated my life to Him that I might be the grandmother, mother, daughter, sister, sister-in-law, daughter-in-law, friend, and neighbor that I should be because of this heritage of someone caring. In years to come, my family and grandchildren will have a deep sense of a godly, dedicated grandparent who had a concern and a vision of passing on this unspeakable gift. I shared this with the congregation that morning and there were tears in many an eye.

"To shake a hand and to look into the faces of relatives you have heard about and are distantly related to you immediately seem as one because of the blood tie, and the spiritual experience is wonderful. After church, Abraham was greeting everyone and then we sat down to a delicious meal with all the Norwegian goodies. Many more meetings were held that day and the following day in the school house and then we boarded the boat to return to America to resume the responsibilities of inspiring the leadership. The Viking returned to America with a new strength, and increased vision and the encouragement and supporting prayers of his own people who remain living on the mountain that their Abraham might go forth to conquer mountains for their Lord and his."

25 | FORWARD

Bermuda, Billings, Montana, and a thousand acre farm in New Hampshire have been the latest scenes of I.C.L. in action; but they are something more. They are a blueprint for future action. They are laymen in action—vision, guidance, teamwork, boldness, and go-to-it. The old general is here, out in front of his troops, calling them on, lifting their sights to new horizons; but at least at Billings it was the troops without the general; and there lies the future of I.C.L.—generals pass on but *The* General abides forever—within His troops; and in each of these three places the troops had the initiative, the troops planned the assault, the troops went into action.

In Bermuda a well-known "drunk," a businessman, gets freed through Christ—through chain reaction. An American visitor, Kay Roberts, herself the wife of a transformed alcoholic, witnesses to him. Harold Cooper, in turn, now gets after all the alcoholics he hears of in the Island. Howard Dickinson, Rhodes scholar and doctor, starts a Bible and sharing group in his home. Geoffrey Kitson, formerly the youngest Commander in the Royal Navy, now at the center of the tourist trade in Bermuda, finds Christ at Madison Square Garden; another group is formed and a business men's lunch. Jack Davies and other men of affairs on the Island join with him.

Fired by what they see happening in Washington as they attend the I.C.L. conference, and at Pocono in the "Faith-at-Work" conferences, they propose to Vereide an invasion of witness in Bermuda.

Faith-at-Work, originally stemming from the Life-Changing ministry of Sam Shoemaker and Irving Harris at Calvary Church at New York, is a fellowship which has now broadened out into an ever-widening movement of lay participation and witness within the churches of all denominations. Many hundreds are being quickened into new life in Christ through it, both inside and outside the churches; some whole congregations, ministers and members, become "participating churches." Its main activities are its magazine of witness called *Faith at Work,* its visiting teams and its weekend conferences, the best known of which is its tremendous annual weekend in the Pocono Mountains of Pennsylvania. Irving Harris, Bruce Larson and Sherry Day, with their teammates and office staff at 8 West 40th Street, New York City, are the hub of a movement which is spreading through the churches of the nation. I.C.L. with its boldness of outreach in the political, professional, and business world, and Faith-at-Work with its penetration into the grass roots of church life, form an excellent partnership.

Vereide's answer is the general's touch, "Yes," says he, "so long as you go for the top. Book the ballroom of a large hotel. Arrange banquets by invitation, one for the politicians, one for the professional men, one for business men. Get the bishop interested. Invite him to come and see for himself what God is doing at the Presidential Breakfast, then ask him to arrange a welcome service in the Cathedral. Book the theater for a public meeting on Sunday evening."

Abram and his daughter, Alicia, arrive in Bermuda a few days before the Conference starts, and they do not wait for the Conference to get busy witnessing. A Norwegian vessel docks at Hamilton, someone brings the second in command of the ship, an alcoholic, to a fellowship luncheon. Alicia accompanies her father back to the ship with this man where, she says, after a conversation, both the captain and this man are on their knees in the cabin with Abram. When they arise, tears are running down the man's face as he tells how he had a praying mother and only that day had been thinking of her, when "God sends you along." Abram then goes down to the seamen's quarters and speaks to the whole crew in Norwegian. When the boat sails the next morning, the crew are lined up on the deck waving signal flags accompanied by blasts from the whistle, with Abram answering from the hotel by waving a shirt and a towel!

The team gets going, all to plan. The bishop warmly cooperates and invites the ministers of other denominations to share the opening service. The cathedral is filled. The theater is packed. The banquets at the Princess Hotel are attended by about two-hundred guests each night. Over a hundred visitors come from the U.S.A. Speakers include a great variety of personal witnesses to Christ; senators, society women, a former actress, presidents of companies, congressmen, lawyers, doctors, an economist, a garage proprietor . . . . Each morning there are intensive group meetings on the key to Christian living, each evening the witnessing continues for at least two hours at the banquets. Free time is given on the radio and television to explain what the campaign is all about. For the last night invitations are given to all who were guests at the previous banquets to come again, paying their own expenses if they felt they would like more. Two hundred and eighty come and others have to be turned away. The large lounge of the hotel has never before, we are sure, witnessed what it did that night, people in all corners, in couples, in groups, doing business with God and making personal commitments to Jesus Christ. There are many open conversions to Christ, right up to the airport where the delay of the plane gave others time to make their peace with God. And the aftermath . . . . the house groups so enlarged that new ones have had to start, more conversions by "chain-reaction," churches with increased attendance, a spiritual quickening in the Island; and one further stride of faith by the same group who first suggested the campaign.

During the meetings God spoke to Howard Dickinson about starting a permanent Christian guest house in the Island for the crowds of visitors for Christians to get spiritual as well as physical renewal, and for non-Christians to be drawn to Christ. At one of the morning talks, he got such definite assurance from God about this that he publicly spoke "the word of faith" —that God had called him to open such a place on the Island and would send the finances necessary. Several hotels were looked at but finally Willow Bank was bought, a furnished house on a lovely stretch of land in Somerset with its own beaches, formerly belonging to an American general. About a quarter of the price was received in gifts. The plan of faith is to build extensions until over one hundred guests can be accommodated. There was an official opening, and later a reception for His Excellency the Governor, the Speaker of the House, the Members of Parliament, business leaders and others. A staff of four are running it for the Lord, without salary. The building enlargements have already begun through the enthusiasm and assistance of a Christian contractor. A Board of businessmen meet weekly for prayer and consultation, themselves sharing sacrificially in the financial obligations at the start. As Canon Wallace Bird of England said at one of the banquets, "Doors move on small hinges. Tens of thousands of visitors come yearly to Bermuda. A vital Christian witness in the Island can make Bermuda a hinge on the door of a world-wide revival."

What happened at Billings, Montana, is what can happen in any city where the Spirit of God is at work in some men's hearts. A Christian young man, Louis Kramp by name, one Sunday picked up in the pew of his church some literature on I.C.L. Breakfast Groups. He was suddenly fired with the desire to see a work of the Spirit in their city. He called together other young laymen, doctors, businessmen, lawyers. William Jones, an attorney and chairman of this group, spoke of them as "a bunch of us who didn't have much in common except an interest in Christian living, but we decided to start having little prayer and discussion meetings." Someone suggested they contact Dick Halverson of I.C.L. Washington about having a week of meetings. Dick got in touch with Ford Mason, the president of the Gum Machine Co. who had previously used his plane to take a team of witness to the various state capitals enroute to Seattle, and asked him if he would fly a team to Billings. This he did, and several other business laymen flew up at their own expense to join them, some from long distances. Among these were W. C. Jones, a publisher from Los Angeles; Jack Johnson, president of a land development company in Oklahoma; Arnold Palmer, manufacturer of baby buggies; George Gardner, an auto dealer of Binghamton, N.Y.; Bill Yinger, in the oil business in Oklahoma; John Young in land development in Florida; and Keith Miller. Dr. Hagerstrom, who met the team on arrival, announced that, in the boldness of faith, they had booked the largest banquet hall in the city at the Northern Hotel and issued invitations at $1.25 a piece to any business man who could come to a 6:30 A.M. breakfast the next morning. They had no idea how many would really come, although two hundred had accepted. At 6:30, two hundred and forty-five were there. The breakfasts were to be continued each morning in the week, and each morning more men were there, sometimes to overflowing and standing in hallways to listen. Nothing was given but plain witness by businessmen to businessmen. The effect was atomic. The wives were so stirred by what they heard from their husbands that they demanded evening services which they could attend. There were many outright conversions, personal conversations continuing with team members till past midnight, although they had to be up for the next morning's breakfast. Men opened their homes and asked the team members to come to speak. A doctor got about thirty other doctors to come. The wealthiest man in the city, with whom Ford Mason had had a private conversation and to whom he had presented a Bible, wrote that the meetings had "a tremendous impact on the business and professional men of Billings in the interests of Christianity, and that the effect would be permanent." Over one thousand different Billings men attended, and the week after the team had left, one hundred fifty men had registered their desire to continue the meetings and to meet for Bible study. Men drove up to two hundred fifty miles to attend the meetings, and some of the team were taken to speak at neighboring cities. Even the breakfasts in the hotel were of unusual standard, for the chef himself was a Christian and a member of the local team! The preachers became stirred and interested as they heard what was going on.

It is good to note again that I.C.L. here was not depending on any one man. Vereide did not take part in the Billings campaign. The invitation did not come *from* I.C.L., but to it. It was local young men who had the vision and took action, and these same young men of Billings are now speaking of contacting others in other cities who might be interested. The men who formed the team were business men who took time off to do it at a sacrifice. Here lies the future of I.C.L. There seems nothing to stop any man in any city with vision and boldness of faith calling for such teams and making the preparations for them.

Gray Ledges is a thousand acre farm overlooking a wonderful panorama of New Hampshire's beautiful mountains and woodlands. The rambling old house was built by a former attorney general of the state two hundred years ago. Mrs. Carol

Sturgis of Plymouth, Massachusetts, the present owner, made a full commitment of her life to Christ three years ago through the witness of Alicia Abrahamsen. The vision then came to her of making Gray Ledges a center of Christian Fellowship and witness for New England. In consultation with Mr. Vereide and her father, Herbert Avery, a retired attorney, she made over the property to a Gray Ledges Association, affiliated with I.C.L. That has not lessened her personal involvement in the project, for a call of God always means, "I'll do it through *you*," and she is in process of completing improvements on the building costing thousands of dollars, usually without the cash in hand for the heavy weekly payments and proving the faithfulness of God each time a bill has to be met. Gray Ledges can at present accommodate twenty-six and is available as a vacation or conference center, while plans are in hand for extensions and additional accommodations.

To sit with Abram on the veranda overlooking those green miles of hills and forests, together with Carol, her father, and others, praying and catching a glimpse of God's plan for this new venture, was like being with the general of an invading army. It was not quiet Gray Ledges that Abram was seeing. It was New England. "Let Gray Ledges be a training center," he said. "Find individuals, first in each state capital, who will be corraling agents to bring people here. God will do a work in those men and women, meet their own needs, and touch minds and hearts with the call for responsible leaders in each city, and have teams of witness to visit state capitals, calling people to prayer, repentance, and Christian action both on a civic level, and in winning men to Christ. It is not to expand I.C.L. that matters; it is Christ for the individual, Christ for the nation, Christ for the world."

"But let the Christian witness start where we are," he continued. "You have near neighbors at Gray Ledges, on the farm, in the little town of Grantham. You have the contractor in charge of the building alterations,the workmen, the man on the farm. Get these interested in serving God by making Gray Ledges a center of blessing for the community." Abram had already talked with the contractor and arranged to meet him and others for a talk on the Gray Ledges project, and that would also mean a witness to Christ.

"Then let the minister in the Grantham church know that we are here to help. Blessing in the community will mean blessing and increase in his church. Attend the services, find out who are Christians in the community and invite them to Gray Ledges and share our witness with them. Let heaven come down through the Bible and testimony. After Pentecost it says the Early Church had 'found favor with all the people.' Our Christian life and witness at Gray Ledges must be like that—winsome, attractive." And Abram turned to one and another as various local families were mentioned; "*You* visit so-and-so; make friends, be a good listener as they unload their problems, win them to Christ; and *you*, so-and-so, and *you*, so-and-so," and finally, "Visit that large house down in the valley; we shall need them as we need room for an overflow!"

Was that merely the talk of a visionary? What has happened in Bermuda and Billings will happen here. God is on the march, and there are plain evidences that I.C.L. is moving into another phase of God's plan for it. The first was God preparing and finding a man who could be His mouthpiece to the political, industrial, and civic leaders of the nation, and to whom they would listen and respond. The second was the establishment of the center in the nation's capital, with the Breakfast Groups in the Senate and House of Representatives, the Presidential Prayer Breakfast, the building of the inner team and all the activities at Fellowship House. The third was the international expansion of the I.C.L. witness in Europe, India, and other countries, and more recently to the leadership of the newly independent nations of Africa. The fourth is the distinct sharpening and urgency in the use of the weapon of team witness; it is the team taking more of the place of one man, and the one man being the prime instigator of this. And it is not merely team witness as a vague generality, but it is a burning vision of the immediacy and practicality of lay witness teams in action all over this country and thus equally all over the world. Mobilize for team witness! and, mobilize for lay team witness,—the man in the street to the man in the street, the Gospel in everyday language to the users of everyday language. Let the layman arise (the Church of Christ is laymen, and the laymen are all ministers, I Peter 2:9.) Let what two young men at Billings did be repeated all over the place. Let laymen who have a witness to give of Christ's power in their lives be ready to put aside weekends and travel here and there by quick, modern transportation, and make the financial sacrifices necessary in order to form such mobile teams of witness. And let the wives give their husbands willingly. Let breakfast groups and fireside groups be formed where Bible study and prayer on a sharing and fellowship level can help build those newly-committed in Christ and keep the older ones on the firing line.

"Lengthen the cords, strengthen the stakes, enlarge the place of thy tent, for thy children shall break forth on the right hand and on the left."

26 | GOD IN ACTION

This has been the story of a man—and a man's man. Nobody embodies perfection. All have the defects of their virtues, and like any other adventurer for God, Abraham Vereide has not been immune from criticism. A common complaint has been that I.C.L. is not definite enough in its message, and therefore not productive enough of really Christ-committed lives.

There is some truth in this. The largeness of Abram Vereide's heart, the breadth of his vision, the positiveness of his outreach which fans the faintest spark of faith in a man rather than quenching it, the expectation of response from men who bear responsibility to their need of a Higher Power to direct them, the conviction that God has a purpose of grace to fulfill in this present world through a leadership led by God—all these have made him more inclusive in those he welcomes into I.C.L. activities than a more strictly and solely "evangelistic" approach would do. That has been the genius of the Spirit in Abraham Vereide. None can claim a more strictly Biblical, orthodox, Christ-centered faith than his, nor a greater love for men and zeal to win them for Christ. But his approach has been specialized, and can anyone say that any other approach would have been more effective? We should be foolish to say so, for the simple fact is that this is the way that God has done it through His servant, and He has not done the same through any other!

God knows His own business. If Abram is immersed in his great outreach, if the love of God in him would daringly compass a class of people by-passed by others, at the same time, God quietly surrounds him with those who are evangelical and evangelistic to the core, and who would never remain in a movement which had any other ultimate objective than to bring people to Christ and to a God-used life—his own daughter Alicia, Wallace Haines, Dick Halverson, Doug Coe, Bill Bullard.

Here is the hope of the future. Yet the delicate balance must be maintained. A too exclusively straight evangelical approach would undoubtedly close doors now opened. Yet too inclusive an approach can have wide open doors that lead to nowhere. Doubtless Abram has grown with his ministry as all do, and by the gradual addition of his co-workers and by his own inner guidance and conviction, I.C.L. has become more definitive. Perhaps it will grow yet more so: perhaps it can, now that it is so widely and internationally recognized and accepted.

Team work is another phase which needs development. Again, it has not been Abram's strong point. This is not because of unwillingness, for there can be no more humble team member than Vereide, but because his gifts and calling are of another kind. The answer to the future of I.C.L. seems to lie here. It is God's usual way—to raise up a founder, and then later a team to be corporately what he was individually, yet with a plus of their own. The team is there, learning and growing.

But the point of all this—of this book, of Abram, and of I.C.L.—is neither I.C.L., nor Vereide, nor his co-workers, nor the problem of present or future, nor finances (which we have not touched upon in the book because, though real enough and necessary enough, they are a secondary, not primary issue). The point is *God Himself*.

The Apostle Paul wrote with thankfulness that "it pleased God, who separated me from my mother's womb, and called me by His grace, to reveal his Son in me, that I might preach him among the heathen."

So it is God Himself who brings people into the world for one purpose only—that they may discover that their real self is not their deluded self-reliant, self-existent, self-acting, self-seeking self: their real self is another Self, another Person living in them and functioning by them; and that Person is Jesus Christ.

Such a fact—an indwelling Christ as the real Self in us—is the only possible remedy for humanity which has got out of gear and deified itself, because this same Jesus Christ became a man, one of us, a human representative, and voluntarily died and rose again in our stead. By dying as our representative, He brought to an end on our behalf this sin-centered life, this life we live by nature under the control of the spirit of self-centeredness: and by rising from the dead on our behalf, by the entry of the Spirit of God into His dead body ("being put to death in the flesh, but quickened by the Spirit," I Peter 3:18), He was the first of a new humanity. This new humanity consists of millions of people who have, as the motivating center of their personalities, not the spirit of self-centeredness which invaded and united itself to humanity through the disobedience of Adam, but the Spirit of self-giving, the Spirit of God, God Himself, Christ Himself living in them. And we are all among these millions, when we have been awakened to our emptiness, helplessness, and sinfulness in our natural condition, and have heard with the inner ear the Gospel of this free gift of God in Jesus Christ, and have simply received and recognized it as a fact for ourselves now: that in actual fact we went to the Cross with Him two thousand years ago, for He was only there as humanity's representative, and in actual fact we rose with Him by the new Spirit, God's Spirit coming into Him and therefore into us: and that, therefore, just here and now I thankfully welcome Him to live in me as a fact, which includes the forgiveness and blotting out of all my past transgressions in the total efficacy of His atoning sacrifice. God who "separated me from my mother's womb" has "revealed His son in me."

For what purpose? That I might now know that I am "called by His grace" to "preach Him among the heathen." In other words, that the One I now recognize as living in me, the real Other Self in me, is a world Lover, a world Saviour, and has a world-saving purpose: and that just as the Spirit in Jesus on earth lived a world-saving life through Him and constrained Him to lay down His life for the world, so that same Spirit in us, that same Christ in us, now lives in our bodies with a world-saving purpose, and constrains us to lay down our lives for the world.

How does that work out in practice? In the simplest possible way. Every human life, when God-possessed in this way, is God-in-action. That ordinary life you and I live is He living it. The circumstances, the environment, the people with whom we are surrounded, the responsibilities large or small, are God's plan, God's special arena of self-revelation. It is not a matter of looking out on others, such as Abraham Vereide, the subject of this book, and saying, "If I were like him, or where he is, I could take part in a world-witness." It is a matter of saying, "My situation, as it is now, *is* God's environment for me, God's calling, God's place of potential Self-manifestation. Let me recognize Him, therefore, in me in this existing situation. Let me catch a glimpse of how He intends to manifest His redemptive love through me, and is already doing so."

Remember Paul again, born with a purpose, receiving the revelation of Christ in him—Why? Because he was called to preach Him among those who didn't know Him. And that is exactly where you and I are. Born for a purpose. Christ revealed in us, as we have received and believed God's word of saving grace to us. Now called—just where we are and as we are—to manifest this same Christ to others in our homes, business, social relationships, in the conduct of our affairs, in the decisions we have a share in making, in the handling of other lives over whom we have control.

Start looking at life from that angle. Open your eyes to Christ in you. Open your ears to His plan and purpose: and soon you will find your own calling to the obediences of faith, to the adventures of faith, such as we have seen in Abram Vereide. You will find the Spirit of God in you saying, "Let us go further. I am in you to love others through you and show them that I am love, and that Jesus is the way, the truth and the life. Believe me now that I intend to do this by you. As I tell you what to do, you obey and do it. You will find the power to speak and act in you (I in you), as you just go along with me in what may seem impossible situations." And as you do this, horizons will enlarge, faith will increase, God will be expanding Himself through you.

Will it cost? Well, if you call it cost—yes. But you don't notice the cost, when you are caught up in the glory of the adventure. "Looking unto Jesus . . . who for the joy that was set before Him endured the cross, despising the shame." All men pay for what they value. Men don't scale Mt. Everest without paying a price, but to them, reaching the summit is worth anything. How much more we, who are climbing the summit of summits —to bring the whole world to the feet of Him who, as we do come, takes us by the hand, lifts us up, and then says, "Now then you go out, with Me in you, to be a world lover and world saviour along with Me and the rest of us. Redeemed to be a redeemer. Saved to be a saviour."

That is the story of Abraham Vereide's life, and the history and reason for the existence of International Christian Leadership. *God* came into that shepherd-boy's heart. *God* took him ways by which he could realize the release that was his in Christ from the bondages of self-reliance, self-seeking, self-gratification. *God* began to express His saving love and concern for the world through that released personality: first among fellow immigrants, then among humanity's wreckage, finally —at the opposite end of the pole—among those who face the greater judgment because they hold the greater responsibility, and therefore have the greater need of the God of wisdom and mercy.

Wallace Haines, writing of Abram from France, says: "I see the visionary in the prophet. He cannot always bring it down to reality. But no one can inspire men as he does. He is a symbol over here. Just what tired, disillusioned Europe needs —and just the mystic for India and just the loving heart for Africa."

Sam Shoemaker wrote: "How wonderfully God has used him with many of the great of the world. So few can get through to them simply and on a real basis, without trading on it or treating them too much like something beside human beings with needs like all the rest of us."

Billy Graham cabled on the twentieth anniversary of the start of the first breakfast group in Seattle: "Abraham Vereide has contributed more to encourage spiritual leadership than any man I know. He is the personification of a Christian gentleman. He is a close personal friend and advisor. Congratulations on Twentieth Anniversary—May God continue to bless this giant of the Christian Faith."

President Eisenhower, when visiting Paris, was asked by Minister of Justice Michelet if he knew Mr. Vereide, and his answer was "Indeed I do. He is a wonderful man, doing a great work."

Were these things said of a mere man? No. they were basically tributes to God in a man—and the glory of God's grace is that He is no respector of persons: it can be God in any man who hears, believes, obeys.

Abram tells of this incident when he paid his first visit to Washington, D.C. in 1913. "I visited with Dr. Diserud, head of the Library of Congress, and I told him that there was one man in Washington I wanted to see more than anybody else. 'Oh, you mean the President,' said he. 'No,' said I. 'I want to see the man whom presidents, regardless of party, and statesmen both at home and abroad, go to for counsel and guidance more than anybody else.' 'Oh,' he burst out, 'you mean Senator Knute Nelson from Minnesota!' 'Yes,' I said, and he took the telephone and made an appointment for me to see him. After a brief visit about politics and state affairs, I asked Senator Nelson this question. 'Tell me, Senator, what is the secret of your great influence and wisdom?' He turned around in his swivel chair and looked out his office window for a few moments of reflection, and then he turned about and said, 'Mr. Vereide—two things. First, when I was a young man, a preacher presented the claims of Christ to me and asked me to yield my life to Jesus Christ, accepting Him as my Savior and Lord. I responded, and stepped forward to the altar and gave the preacher my hand and Christ my heart. That is number one. Number two'—he pulled out the drawer of his desk and took out a well-worn Bible, saying, 'You see this Book? This is the inspiration and guide for my life. His Word is a lamp unto my feet, and a light unto my pathway. The entrance of His Word gives life.'"

There lies the secret.

EPILOGUE

THE 1961 BREAKFAST

With the election of a new President, could there be a continuation of the Presidential Prayer Breakfast? Vereide had no doubt about it. "He will come," he said by faith as soon as the results of the election were announced; and he was right. Not only did the President come, but the Vice President, the second time both had attended together, and a larger number of the members of the new Cabinet than ever before: Secretary of State Dean Rusk, Secretary of Treasury Dillon, Secretary of Defense Macnamara, Secretary of Agriculture Freeman, Secretary of Labor Goldberg, Secretary of Commerce Hodges, Postmaster General Day, and Adlai Stevenson, Ambassador to the United Nations, who flew down from New York for the occasion.

David Lawrence in an editorial in the New York Herald Tribune and Washington Evening Star called it "A milestone religious event." Dr. Frederick Brown Harris, Chaplain of the United States Senate, wrote in the Sunday Star: "It is no exaggeration to declare that on February 9, the most vitally important spot in the free world . . . was a room in Washington, D.C. It is a spacious golden room and in it at 8:00 o'clock in the morning many hundred Americans sat down to break bread, to meditate and to pray. Just across the corridor were almost 800 women having their own service for the same purpose. The President of the United States was there—and the Vice President, members of the Cabinet, officials of the Pentagon, members of the Supreme Court, Senators and members of the House, judges, and other prominent citizens from all walks of life. They were there as men of religious faith at the call of International Christian Leadership to acknowledge that the spiritual verities by which we live, and by which alone we can conquer, are the most potent asset of our national strength— . . . [and] gathered to think together regarding the total mobilization of all the spiritual forces of the Republic."

Dr. Billy Graham addressing the Breakfast.

Dr. Billy Graham, President Kennedy, Sen. Frank Carlson, and Judge Boyd Leedom bow their heads during the invocation at the Presidential Prayer Breakfast 1961.

"There are no words," he continued, "to convey the deep religious content of that hour. In so much that was said and sung, there resounded the assurance framed by Frances Havergal—'Reality, reality, Jesus Christ I find in thee.' More and more as the world crisis deepens, Americans of all church traditions are ready to confess that in this land where freedom has so often degenerated into license, something terrible is happening to the once flaming beliefs of the Pilgrims built into the very foundations of the Republic. Also it must be confessed that it is often with a bleached and anaemic creed that we face the catastrophic situation of these fearful days.

"We are mobilizing our national might to meet the mailed impact of overwhelming numbers whose fanatical creed thunders around the world, but rises no higher than the dust beneath humanity's feet. Unless the 'I believe' of the free world has back of it the invincible assets of which atheistic materialsim is impoverished, we face a future of immeasurable gloom.

"At this annual prayer breakfast America was summoned to its knees that it might recapture a sense of the divine undergirding. This 'under God' consciousness which is gripping so many of our anxious leaders has, of course, no partisan implications. Here, in 1961, was held one of the most amazing prayer meetings ever held since George Washington agonized on the frozen ground of Valley Forge."

The U.S. News and World Report called it "A morning of prayer in politically hardened Washington, an impressive occasion when the top ranks of government—Democrats and Republicans—put political differences aside to join in a devotional meeting."

President Kennedy was the last to speak, after Billy Graham had given his address. It was evident, as the audience rose to applaud him when he returned to his seat, that the simplicity and sincerity of what he said had made its impact—this personal affirmation of faith by the new President in the presence of so many hundreds of those who are to govern the nation these next four years under his leadership.

In his four minute speech the President said: "I think it's most appropriate that we should be gathered together for this morning's meeting. This country was founded by men and women who are dedicated to two propositions: first, a strong religious conviction, and second, a recognition that this conviction could flourish only under a system of freedom. I think it is appropriate that we pay tribute to this great constitutional principle which is enshrined in the first ammendment of the Constitution, the principle of religious freedom. But I think it is also important that we pay tribute to and acknowledge another great principle, and that is the principle of religious conviction. Religious freedom has no significance unless it is accompanied by conviction . . . No man who enters upon the Office to which I have succeeded can fail to recognize how every President of the United States has placed special reliance upon his faith in God. Every President has taken comfort and courage when told as we are told today, that 'the Lord will be with thee. He will not fail thee nor forsake thee' . . . We must recognize that human collaboration is not enough, that in times such as these we must reach beyond ourselves if we are to seek ultimate courage and infinite wisdom. It is an ironic fact that in this nuclear age, when the horizon of human experience has passed far beyond any that any age has ever known, we turn back in this time to the oldest source of wisdom and strength, to the words of the prophets and saints who tell us that faith is more powerful than doubt, that hope is more potent than despair, and that only through love that is sometimes called charity, can we conquer those forces within ourselves and throughout all the world that threaten the very existence of mankind, keeping in mind that 'when a man's ways please the Lord, he maketh even his enemies to be at peace with him.' "

Vice President Lyndon Johnson referred to the relations between religion and government which had stirred up so many questions during the election period. "In recent months," he said, "our nation has re-examined and reaffirmed the principle of church and state. We cherish that principle and the protection it affords the integrity of each man's soul. I am sure the principle has no stronger defender than the man who sits with us here this morning as the President of the United States. But we need to remember that the separation of church and state must never mean the separation of religious values from the lives of our public servants. In our nation's earliest history

William Penn warned us that if we will not be governed by God, then we must be governed by tyrants. If we who serve free men today are to differ from the tyrants of that age, we must balance the powers in our hands with God in our hearts. America need fear no man who fears God, and the nation that fears God need fear no man . . . we can have no real sense of responsibility in our public lives unless we have a real spirit of reverence in our private lives. These times often require responsible men to forget their politics, but never their prayers. Every public servant is tallest on his knees."

From the start of the program, after the eating of the breakfast to its close, the atmosphere was almost like an evangelistic meeting. The Army Choir brought us into God's presence by the singing of "Sweet Hour of Prayer," in which every word could be distinctly heard, all the more impressive when sung by that company of young men in their military uniforms.

The Metropolitan Opera Singer, Jerome Hines, prefaced his solo by a word of witness which obviously captured the surprised attention of the President, who had just remarked to Billy Graham sitting next to him that he had often heard Hines sing. "Mr. President, our guests," he said, "I'm not here today to sing for the President, though it's an honor. I'm here for one purpose and that's to tell you what happened to me eight years ago and what's been happening ever since. I have found the greatest Friend in the world. I found Jesus Christ, and the thing I want to tell everybody all the time is that Jesus Christ is not just a philosophy to live by. He is that same living Person that was resurrected two thousand years ago. I know Jesus Christ and I know Him in my heart. I know Him personally and Jesus Christ has told me that I am his son, that I am saved, that I belong to Him because He bought me at the price of His own sacrifice upon the cross. I have that blessed assurance. in my life. That's what my song is going to be today." Hines then sang, not some great operatic classic, but the simple old time favorite, "Blessed Assurance, Jesus is Mine."

W. C. Jones, the Los Angeles publisher, who was the host of the Breakfast, instead of giving a word of welcome, followed Hines in capturing the attention of the audience by a brief outline of his life story. He told how when twenty-two years of age he owned five newspapers, "but there was still a vacuum.

Something was still missing. I saw people going to the horse races, and they looked like they were having a better time than I was, so I joined them. When I reached the age of twenty-eight I had drunk away all my friends, gambled away my business, and the nicest thing you could say was that I was a hopeless drunk. I started in again and this time I thought, *Well, maybe if I give some money to the church, this would be Christian service.* I gave $25.00 a week in 1941, got up to $800.00 a month in 1950 and I was still just as far from finding reality in my life. In 1952 my wife and I were to be divorced. The love in our home had gone dead. Then suddenly I realized that money couldn't buy everything. I would have given everything I had, if I could just get this love back. My wife and I knelt and asked Christ to come into our hearts and a miracle happened. The reason I am so certain is because that night the taste for liquor left, never to come back again. Our home was brought together. We fell in love again. God poured so much love into our home, we had to adopt five children to share it with. I would never go to church; now I go to church because I want to. Whereas I could never discuss Jesus Christ before, He is now the most important person in my vocabulary. Mr. President, you would be thrilled to see our five children as we gather each day and form a partnership with you in your duties. We pray every night that God will give you the wisdom to guide this nation."

The whole audience rose, as they did for the President, when Billy Graham went to the speaker's rostrum, the first to rise being the President himself. Graham spoke with his usual directness, on "heart trouble" being the root problem facing the human race today, with the Biblical estimate of the heart as deceitful and wicked above all things, the hopelessness of trying to legislate morals or love, but how Jesus Christ came "to give His heart and die on the cross"; and that in all his travels he could see no possibility that human nature can be radically changed apart from the power of that cross. "God says, 'I am willing to give you a new heart,' and that's what Christ meant when he said, 'Except a man be born again he cannot see the kingdom of heaven.' And whoever you are today struggling with your own personal problems, sin, temptation, and difficulties, I tell you that Jesus Christ has the

Abraham Vereide with President Kennedy, Sen. Carlson, Billy Graham, and Vice President Lyndon Johnson.

The Congressional Wives' Breakfast at the Mayflower Hotel, Washington, Feb. 9, 1961. (l. to r.) Mrs. Samuel Shoemaker, Mrs. Olin B. Johnston, Chairman; President Kennedy, Vice President Johnson, Dr. Graham, Mrs. Lyndon B. Johnson, the guest of honour, C. J. Mack, Representative Frances Bolton of Ohio, Dr. Vereide, and Colonel Mary Louise Milligan, Director of the Womens' Army Corps. Lady in foreground—Mrs. Elizabeth Iglehart.

Photos by Seth Muse

power to change your life." He closed by saying, "I think it is highly significant that the President and Vice President and members of the Cabinet, Senate, and Congress should be here at this hour, joining hands with governors throughout the nation to look to God. I am certain that this pleases the court of heaven and without His help this nation is doomed. I believe, Mr. President, that in the new frontier with which you have challenged us all, there is also its spiritual and moral undergirding. I believe that once again God has given this nation a new opportunity under the leadership of our new President."

After Abraham Vereide had prayed the closing prayer, the chairman, Senator Carlson, asked the President (and raised a laugh in doing so) if he would spare a moment to visit 600 ladies who were meeting in another room of the hotel. This was the first Congressional Wives' Prayer Breakfast, arranged by Marian Adair and Alicia Abrahamsen, with Mrs. Olin Johnston as chairman. The Vice President's wife was the guest of honour. The opening prayer was made by Mary Haworth, the well-known columnist. The Hon. Katharine St. George brought a message, and the main speaker was Helen Shoemaker, the daughter of former Senator Alexander Smith. To these ladies the President said, "It seems to me that in the true Christian spirit next year we should all sit down together, and that we should have gentlemen and ladies pray and reason together, but we are glad we came here—the Vice President and I came under the protection of Dr. Graham." He then referred to some Baptist missionaries from the Congo, India, and Korea, who had recently visited him at the White House, and said: "We must match that faith. We must demonstrate in our lives . . . that we care deeply," like those "who have been willing to spend their lives under the most difficult circumstances, in great hardship, in order to carry the message in which they have such great conviction."

The ladies' meeting continued for two and one-half hours on the subject "Women whom God can use," with a stream of witness to Christ from women in various walks of life, led by Eleanor Whitney, Dorothy Broger, Elizabeth Inglehart, Kay Roberts, Darlene Swanson, and others. As one listener said later, "I couldn't get over all these society women speaking about Jesus Christ." A U.S. Congressman wrote concerning the

Presidential Breakfast to Douglas Coe: "No spiritual experience has made a greater impact upon me, and I am confident that the results of the meeting will long be felt in the Halls of Congress and throughout the land. Truly God has used the occasion to speak to America and it is my hope that His Word will reach into the hearts of men and that we may move nearer to our destiny with Him."

The year 1961 has been one of 'a new frontier' for I.C.L. The proposal to arrange governors' prayer breakfasts in the various States received such an encouraging response ("There just wasn't any negative response," said Doug Coe), that thirty were held this year, and in 1962 every state with only two or three exceptions is to have one. The average attendance has been three hundred. The legislature in one state immediately passed a resolution that the breakfast should be held each year. In Boston, where four-hundred-fifty attended, Carol Sturgis, who was largely responsible for organizing it, wrote: "God's Holy Spirit pervaded that room and hearts were deeply touched. Over half were Catholics and the priest who gave the benediction said in all his years in Boston he had never been so deeply touched by any occasion. With tears in his eyes and voice he said he praised God that we could meet and eat together in worship of the same Lord Jesus Christ."

One legislator wrote that all his life he had been missing something, but did not know till that breakfast that it was Jesus Christ. "The work is moving so rapidly," wrote Alicia Abrahamsen from Washington, "with the letters received after the breakfast, the new groups being formed, the enthusiasm in Bible study shown by the Congressional wives, that it makes your head swim to try to keep up—can't because the Lord is doing it!" Billy Graham was right when he said in his address, "I sense a new spirit in the world," and Abraham Vereide when he stated, "In Christ lies the clue and climax to history."

I.C.L. International Board meeting in Vandenberg Room in the Senate Building. Sen. Alexander Wiley is seated at the head of the table with Sen. Estes Kefauver on his left. Next is Rep. Brooks Hays, then Miss Carrie Lea White, Dr. Vereide's sec'y. Seated on the left are Dr. Edmund Lee, John Broger, Mrs. Alicia Abrahamsen and Thomas R. Wilson. Standing l. to r. are Dr. L. Corea, Rep. Walter H. Judd, Sen. Price Daniel, Dr. Ernest Griffith, Mr. Vereide and Dr. Elgin Groseclose.

Dr. Abraham Vereide and his three sons: Warren, Milton and Abe.

21297

ABOUT THE AUTHOR—

NORMAN GRUBB

Mr. Grubb has been a close friend of Dr. Vereide for more than 15 years. He was an officer in the British Army during World War I and received the Military Cross. After attending Cambridge University, Mr. Grubb joined the famous C. T. Studd, well-known pioneer missionary to the Congo. He is widely known as an author and lecturer in Great Britain and the U.S.A., and is a brother of Sir Kenneth Grubb who was head of the British Ministry of Information during World War II.